GREAT
JUSTICES
of the
SUPREME COURT

GREAT JUSTICES

of the
SUPREME COURT

Nathan Aaseng

illustrated with photographs

The Oliver Press, Inc.
Minneapolis

The Oliver Press
Josiah King House
2709 Lyndale Avenue South
Minneapolis, MN 55408

Library of Congress Cataloging-in-Publication Data

Aaseng, Nathan
Great Justices of the Supreme Court / Nathan Aaseng.

p.   cm. — (Profiles)
Includes bibliographical references and index.
    Summary: Profiles eight notable justices of the United States Supreme Court and landmark cases in which each was involved: John Marshall, Roger Taney, John Harlan, Oliver Wendell Holmes, Louis Brandeis, Charles Evans Hughes, Hugo Black, Earl Warren.
ISBN 1-881508-01-3 : $14.95
1. United States.   Supreme Court—Biography—Juvenile literature.
2. Judges—United States—Biography—Juvenile literature. [1. United States. Supreme Court—Biography.   2. Judges.] I. Title.   II. Series: Profiles   (Minneapolis, Minn.)
KF8744.A18   1992
347.73'26—dc20
[B]
[347.3073534]   92-18443
[B]   CIP
                                                                                   AC

ISBN 1-881508-01-3
Profiles IV
Printed in the United States of America

99 98 97 96 95 94 93 92   8 7 6 5 4 3 2 1

Contents

John Jay (1745-1829), who shared President Washington's belief in a strong central government, became the first chief justice of the Supreme Court. He grew tired of the job, however, and resigned after only six years, in 1795, when he was elected governor of New York.

Introduction

The Supreme Court of the United States limped out of the starting gate on February 1, 1790. Only three of the six justices chosen by President George Washington showed up for the opening session, one short of the number needed to conduct business. A fourth member arrived a day later, only to discover that the Court had no business to conduct.

The Supreme Court could hardly earn the country's respect when even its members did not take it seriously. Chief Justice John Jay spent most of his term traveling overseas. John Blair seldom put in an appearance. John Rutledge resigned in 1791 without ever having attended a session!

When the Court finally handled an important case in 1793, its decision was quickly overruled by voters. In the case of *Chisholm v. Georgia* (Court records shorten versus to v.) the Court upheld the right of citizens of South Carolina to sue the state of Georgia. Within five years, Americans adopted the Eleventh Amendment, which made it illegal for citizens of one state to sue another state. This gave further proof that Alexander Hamilton had been correct in describing the courts as "beyond comparison the weakest" branch of the federal government.

Hidden beneath the limp exterior of the Supreme Court, however, lay two pillars of power just waiting to be discovered. First, in an effort to bolster the Court against the more powerful executive and legislative branches of government, the founders of the United States had given Supreme Court justices unlimited terms. While voters could remove presidents and members of Congress from office, Supreme Court justices were free from the pressure of public opinion.

Second, the Constitution was not clear as to the powers and duties of the Supreme Court. Section 2 of Article III stated that "judicial power shall extend to all Cases, in Law and Equity, arising under this constitution." Readers could interpret that clause to mean a number of things. Many of the early leaders of the United States thought that the Court existed only to settle arguments between states or between the two other branches of government. A few believed that the Supreme Court was the final judge as to whether laws

10

Co-author with John Jay and James Madison of The
Federalist Papers, *Alexander Hamilton (1755-1804) urged
Americans to accept the Constitution, which established the
Supreme Court and gave the federal government more power
than the individual states.*

passed by Congress met the standards set by the
Constitution. Eventually, some people interpreted the
clause to mean that the Constitution gave the Supreme
Court the right to strike down even state laws that it
declared to be unconstitutional.

Beginning in 1801, John Marshall proved that the
combination of unlimited term of office and the vague
language of the Constitution offered the Supreme
Court the power to make a great impact on society. All

that was needed were judges with the courage, vision, and determination to use that power. The following profiles show how eight Supreme Court justices with an abundance of those qualities have left their mark on the United States.

The eight selections reflect the fact that the vast majority of Supreme Court justices have been white, male, and Protestant. As with the United States government in general, the Supreme Court has been slow in breaking down social barriers. The first Roman Catholic justice, Roger Taney, took his seat on the court in 1836. Not until 1916 was a Jew, Louis Brandeis, admitted to this select group. Blacks, or African-Americans, were not represented on the Supreme Court during its first 178 years. In 1967, Thurgood Marshall, a brilliant civil rights lawyer who successfully argued the landmark school desegregation case of *Brown v. The Board of Education of Topeka*, broke that barrier. Women were denied a seat on the High Court until 1981, when Sandra Day O'Connor was approved 99-0 by the United States Senate. Obviously, women and minority groups have had little chance to wield the power of the Supreme Court.

Aware of the potential impact of a first-rate Supreme Court justice, presidents have thought long and hard about the people they have nominated to the Court. Presidents have tried to determine whether their candidates are liberal or conservative—whether their nominees seek an active role for the Court in promoting

12

President Ronald Reagan nominated the first woman to serve on the Supreme Court. Justice Sandra Day O'Connor, a Phoenix lawyer, judge, and former Arizona state senator, joined the Court in September 1981.

social justice or whether they prefer to let the other branches of the government do this job. They have studied court records for clues as to whether their choices believe the Constitution sets strict guidelines or should be open to interpretation.

Some presidents have sought political balance. Republicans, such as William Howard Taft, and Democrats, such as Harry Truman, have appointed members of the opposing political party to the Court. Other presidents have tried to "stack" the Court with justices who agreed with their political views. George

13

Washington and John Adams appointed only Federalists to the Court. Post-Civil War Republicans loaded the Court with supporters of big business. Democrat Franklin Roosevelt and Republican Ronald Reagan used their appointments to tilt the Court to their own views.

But other presidents have not been so successful at doing this. Woodrow Wilson and Dwight Eisenhower were among the many presidents whose nominees ended up opposing them on most issues. Richard Nixon resigned from the presidency after three of his own appointees joined the ruling that he must hand over the White House tapes that incriminated him in the Watergate scandal.

Remarking on the independence shown by Supreme Court justices, Harry Truman once said, "Whenever you put a man on the Supreme Court he ceases to be your friend." One reason for this is that the Supreme Court has become, in the words of Justice Robert Jackson, the "balance wheel" of the government. The Court is responsible for maintaining a working relationship between the states and the federal government and for regulating commerce among the states. It acts as a referee in clashes between presidential and congressional power. The Court stands as the mediator, or umpire, when the power of the government rubs against the rights of individuals.

The enormous responsibility of maintaining the country's balance often gives justices a new perspective on government. When asked if a person changes his views when appointed to the Court, Justice Felix Frankfurter said, "If he is any good he does."

The Supreme Court has long ceased to be a gathering of unwilling appointees. Out of more than 12 million cases clogging the United States courts each year, the Supreme Court rules on 140 to 170 of the most important ones. Its decisions and opinions shape the way our government carries out laws in the country. Largely through the efforts of the eight justices profiled in this book, the Supreme Court now towers as the undisputed guardian of the scales of justice in the United States.

Austrian-born Harvard Law School Professor Felix Frankfurter (1882-1965) shared many liberal views with President Franklin Roosevelt, who nominated him to the High Court, where he served from 1939 to 1962.

John Marshall, known as the Great Chief Justice, did more than anyone else to help the Supreme Court become a major institution of the United States government. He said, ours is "a government of laws, and not of men."

Chapter 1

John Marshall:
Giant of American Law

*A*s the last days of his term slipped away in 1800, President John Adams pondered how to fill the Supreme Court vacancy created by the resignation of Chief Justice Oliver Ellsworth. The president could not persuade John Jay, his first choice, to take the job. Having served briefly as the country's first chief justice, Jay knew how dull and unimportant the post was.

As a second choice, Adams nominated his secretary of state, John Marshall. Within two years, Marshall's forceful personality changed the Supreme Court from a backroom warehouse of leisurely busywork into a furious

Though distant relatives, Thomas Jefferson (above) and John Marshall battled as rivals for many years.

legal battleground. In doing so, he enraged President Thomas Jefferson, who tried to crush Marshall and the Supreme Court with him.

Yet, armed with nothing but his wits against the vast powers of the presidency, Marshall won the battle. Almost single-handedly, he established the Supreme Court as a powerful arm of government and helped to shape a collection of stubbornly independent states into a nation. He accomplished all this despite only one year of formal education and just a few weeks of law school.

John Marshall began life in a log cabin near what is now Fauquier County, Virginia, on September 24, 1755, the first of 15 children born to Thomas and Mary Keith Marshall. Thomas was a poor but well-educated man. His boyhood friendship with George Washington continued into adulthood and brought him into the company of Virginia's most respected families. Mary, a cousin of Thomas Jefferson, was equally familiar with the upper ranks of Virginia society. Yet the Marshalls preferred a simple life on the edge of the Virginia wilderness.

Marshall's fellow Virginian, George Washington, played an important role in his political career.

Young John Marshall enjoyed a wide range of experiences. He grew up eager to learn poetry and fiction from his parents and to tromp through the wilderness with his uneducated friends. John did not attend a formal school until he was 14. A year later his father hired a private tutor who taught John at home. By the age of 18, John had become fascinated with the law, which he studied on his own. The nearest source of law books was an attorney's office 18 miles away. Every few weeks, John hiked across the mountains to borrow more books.

When the British sent troops to put down the rebellious Americans in 1775, John Marshall enlisted in a frontier regiment in Virginia. This group overwhelmed a small British force near Norfolk in December, 1775. As the war spread throughout the colonies, Marshall was commissioned an officer in the newly formed national army led by his father's old friend, George Washington.

The disorder of the American forces exasperated Marshall. Some states refused to cooperate with the national army and tried instead to fight their own battles with their own armies. Poorly equipped and outnumbered, Washington's troops suffered defeats at Brandywine and Germantown and had to abandon the key cities of New York and Philadelphia to the British.

The ragged American army spent the miserable winter of 1777-78 at Valley Forge, Pennsylvania, while states continued to ignore the army's pleas for supplies.

The misery and suffering Marshall saw at Valley Forge helped to influence his belief in the need for a strong, well-organized central government that would provide for its soldiers, rather than leave that task to individual states.

Without clothing, thousands of the soldiers huddled in flimsy shelters throughout the winter. As he watched his fellow soldiers starve and die of illness, Marshall longed for a strong central government to keep the states working together as one nation. "I went into the Revolution a Virginian and came out an American," he once said.

Marshall's cheerful spirits and fair leadership earned him an appointment as a deputy judge advocate who helped settle disputes in the army. He remained with the army throughout the heaviest fighting and then returned home at the end of 1779. Marshall enrolled in a law course at the College of William and Mary but quit after five weeks when his girlfriend, Mary Willis Ambler, moved to Richmond with her family. Marshall followed them and started a law practice in Richmond at about the time the main British force surrendered in 1781. In 1783 John and Mary married.

Popular among war veterans who remembered his leadership, Marshall won election to the Virginia legislature at the age of 27. There he again saw the need for a strong national government. The American forces had signed a treaty that recognized the right of the British to collect debts owed to them by Americans. However, Virginia's laws prevented that collection. Marshall and other people who wanted a strong central government wondered how nations could make treaties or trade agreements with America if some states ignored those agreements.

How could foreign trade be established when each state printed its own money and passed its own trade laws?

Frustrated by the situation, Marshall dropped out of politics. His fine reputation as a lawyer brought him a booming business. Were it not for his sense of duty, Marshall would gladly have kept to private practice. But events changed his life. In 1787, Virginia was evenly split with regard to approving a proposed United States Constitution that would create the kind of national government that Marshall wanted. Running for the legislature so that he could help get the Constitution adopted, Marshall won easily.

Constitution supporters chose Marshall to present their case because of his gift for making legal issues clear to ordinary persons. Despite the opposition of such respected men as Patrick Henry, Virginia approved the Constitution by a vote of 89-79, with the recommendation that a Bill of Rights be added.

Having accomplished his goal, Marshall quit the legislature. During the next decade, Marshall turned down positions as United States attorney general, Supreme Court justice, and ambassador to France.

Marshall contended with forceful speakers such as Patrick Henry (1736-1799) in persuading Virginians to accept the new Constitution.

However, loyalty called him back into the political arena. When President Washington's treaty with Great Britain aroused a storm of protest, Marshall again ran for the Virginia legislature to offer his support to an old family friend. A few years later, he answered the request of President John Adams to negotiate a peace treaty with the French government of Napoleon Bonaparte. Marshall spent a year in France without reaching an agreement. He sailed for home believing his mission a failure. But when he arrived in the United States, Marshall was met with a parade and a welcome "never before given any other American." To his surprise, his firm refusal to pay any bribes demanded by French officials for their cooperation had made him a national hero.

Embarrassed by the fuss, Marshall retreated to private practice. The health of his wife, who suffered from nervous fits through most of their marriage, especially concerned him. But when the Democratic-Republican party of Thomas Jefferson began to win support from the American people near the turn of the eighteenth century, George Washington pleaded with Marshall to run for Congress and to speak out for the crumbling Federalist party. Marshall responded to his family friend's appeal and won a seat in Congress.

In the summer of 1800 Marshall reluctantly agreed to serve as secretary of state in the Adams administration. A few months later, Adams offered him the position of chief justice on the Supreme Court. This was perhaps the one government job that really interested Marshall. Marshall believed that the Supreme Court, contrary to popular opinion at that time, could be an important force in helping to establish consistent, orderly laws to unite all Americans.

Shortly after Marshall took his spot on the Supreme Court, Jefferson defeated Adams in the presidential election. In the days before Jefferson took office, Adams tried to retain power for the Federalists by appointing many new judges. Unfortunately, he did not have time to deliver the commissions to all the newly appointed officials. When Jefferson became president, he ordered his secretary of state, James Madison, to ignore the commissions. Four of the justices who were denied their commissions then sued in federal court. One of the those who filed suit was William Marbury, and the case became known as *Marbury v. Madison*.

By this time, the conflicting political ideas of Chief Justice Marshall and President Jefferson had made them bitter enemies. Marshall, a Federalist, believed that only a strong federal government could protect the liberty of all Americans. In his view, Jefferson was "an absolute terrorist." Jefferson, a Democratic-Republican, disliked all but the most basic government control. He spoke of Marshall as a "twistifier of the law" and "that gloomy malignancy."

When the Supreme Court met to consider the *Marbury v. Madison* case in 1803, Marshall found himself trapped by his rival, the president. If the Court ruled in favor of Marbury, Jefferson would simply ignore the decision. Since the Supreme Court controlled no army or police force, it could not force Jefferson to do anything. Jefferson was such a popular president and the Supreme Court was so lowly regarded by the American people that the president could get away with brushing the ruling aside. That, of course, would demonstrate to the nation that decisions made by the Supreme Court were worthless. On the other hand, if the Federalist Court gave in to the president and ignored the law, the judges would seem spineless. Either way the Supreme Court would lose what little authority and respect it had.

With the future of the Supreme Court on the line, Marshall responded with a stroke of genius. Delivering the Court's opinion himself, he maintained the Court's dignity. First he declared that Marbury was legally entitled to his commission as a justice of the peace. Then he sidestepped Jefferson on a technicality by declaring that, according to the Constitution, Marbury's appeal was not a proper case for the Supreme Court to consider. Although Congress had passed a law that gave the Court the power to issue a legal order in this case, Marshall ruled that this law was invalid. That is, the Constitution did not give Congress the right to grant

26

that power to the Court. Because the congressional action was unconstitutional, it could not be allowed to stand, and the Court could not take the action that Marbury asked.

Marshall's maneuver stunned Jefferson. Never before had the Court claimed it could overrule a law of Congress. In fact, Jefferson did not believe the Supreme Court had the power to do so. Yet Marshall claimed that power in a way that gave Jefferson exactly what he had wanted! The president could not attack a decision that ruled in his favor and against Marbury. He had to let the decision stand even though he hated Marshall's opinion. The Supreme Court emerged from the Marbury trap with more power than ever before!

The Jefferson administration tried other maneuvers to put down this meddlesome Federalist Court. The most drastic strategy involved impeachment—the removal of federal judges by a vote of Congress. Justice Samuel Chase, an outspoken opponent of the Democratic-Republicans, narrowly avoided conviction in an impeachment trial in 1804. Marshall took the hint that the Democratic-Republican party was looking for an excuse to impeach him, too.

He especially felt this during the trial of Aaron Burr in 1807. Burr had been vice-president during Jefferson's first term as president, but the two had since become enemies. Burr had gotten mixed up in a bizarre scheme to gain control of some western land that was under

Aaron Burr (1757-1836), who killed Alexander Hamilton in an 1804 duel, stood trial for treason against the United States after having led a distinguished military and political career.

Spanish rule. Jefferson, claiming that Burr wanted to set up his own empire against the interests of the United States, charged his former vice-president with treason. As chief justice, Marshall had to preside over the trial. The emotionally charged hearing was, in Marshall's words, "the most unpleasant case ever to be brought before a judge."

Marshall was caught in another bind. He knew that Jefferson desperately wanted a conviction and that

Jefferson also wanted to see him impeached. Fairly but firmly, Marshall observed that the writers of the Constitution were distrustful of powerful people who made a charge of treason in order to eliminate opponents. Marshall maintained that in order to convict Burr of treason, the government had to prove that Burr committed acts of war against the United States.

Marshall's opponents raised a howl of protest, but the chief justice insisted that "this court not shrink from its duty." Marshall's ruling stuck, and the Court acquitted Burr. Marshall had handled the case too skillfully to give any cause for impeachment.

The best hope Democratic-Republicans had for bottling up Marshall's influence lay in their judicial appointments. For 24 years, Jefferson and his fellow Democratic-Republican presidents, James Madison and James Monroe, filled every Supreme Court vacancy with judges more in line with their thinking on the issues. Yet Marshall's magnetic personality and clear logic proved difficult for the new appointees to resist. Even those political opponents who denounced Federalists as proud, highborn snobs only concerned with protecting their wealthy friends had to admit that Marshall did not fit the image.

Marshall had little time for glory or for puffed-up language, and he cared nothing for physical appearance. Once Marshall was shuffling along in the street when a well-bred gentlemen mistook him for a lazy common laborer. The gentlemen tossed Marshall a quarter and asked him to carry a live turkey. Rather than bristle at the insult, the chief justice of the Supreme Court trailed behind the man, chuckling to himself as he carried the flapping bird.

Although a man of iron convictions, Marshall bent over backwards to preside evenhandedly over the Court. The chief justice refused to take part in political debates. So determined was he to remain unprejudiced on all issues that he would not even vote in national elections. In leading the Court, he encouraged arguments, listened respectfully to opponents, and when their arguments persuaded him, admitted they were right.

Marshall so impressed his colleagues that he kept winning the Democratic-Republican judges over to his way of thinking. One Madison appointee, Joseph Story, became Marshall's most powerful ally on the Court. Even when Marshall was outnumbered on the Supreme Court by Democratic-Republican justices, the Court voted his way unanimously on most important decisions!

Unlike the Supreme Court that had bored John Jay, Marshall's Court took an active role in forging a jumble of squabbling states into a workable nation. A Court that had seldom heard more than five cases a year before Marshall's arrival, issued more than 11,000 opinions under Marshall's leadership.

30

Nominated to the Supreme Court by President Madison to balance Chief Justice Marshall's strong constitutional views, Joseph Story (1779-1845) soon became a loyal supporter of Marshall. Justice Story served on the Court for 34 years.

One case involved a flip-flop by the Georgia legislature. In the 1790s, dishonest lawmakers sold huge chunks of land in western Georgia and Alabama at a cheap price. When the voters of Georgia discovered what was happening to state land, they angrily voted in a new legislature that took back the land. Land speculators who had suddenly lost their land sued. The

31

Marshall Court ruled that Georgia's new law canceling the land contracts was unconstitutional. "When, then, a law is in its nature a contract, . . . a repeal of the law cannot divest these rights," said Marshall. Although the decision nearly caused a revolt in Georgia, it established that government must respect a person's private property.

In 1819 the case of *Dartmouth College v. Woodward* raised a question of corporate control. Unhappy with the way the college was being run, the New Hampshire state government revised the Dartmouth charter to add new members to the board of trustees. The secretary of the original board reacted by hiding the charter and records. The new board of trustees sued to get the charter back.

The Marshall Court decided in favor of the original board of trustees. The Court ruled that corporations, such as Dartmouth College, had the same rights as individuals under the Constitution. Therefore, the government could not change corporate charters. This protection of corporations from government interference helped to stimulate the industrial development of the United States.

Another important case decided by the Marshall Court concerned an attempt by the state of Maryland to levy a tax against the Bank of the United States. When the national bank refused to pay the tax, the case came before the Supreme Court. Marshall's decision, supported by the other justices, favored the national bank. The

32

Court reasoned that by assuming the power to tax a national institution, the state of Maryland had also assumed the power to destroy that institution. The Court could not allow the national government to be at the mercy of individual states. Marshall declared that national laws, as long as they obeyed the Constitution, took priority over state laws.

Answering Maryland's charge that the Constitution said nothing about the power of Congress to set up a national bank, Marshall laid out the doctrine of "implied powers." According to Marshall, the Constitution does not list all the powers of the national government; rather, it outlines them. The Marshall Court maintained that the national government may assume powers not specifically stated in the Constitution if those powers were "implied" by the Constitution.

Marshall did not win every battle while chief justice. In 1832, two missionaries violated a Georgia law forbidding white people to work without a state permit in Indian territory. The two men appealed to the Supreme Court. The Court ruled in favor of the missionaries on the grounds that Indian relations were questions of national policy and that by taking matters into its own hands, Georgia violated the powers of Congress and the president.

Georgia dared the Court to enforce this ruling. Enforcement of federal law was the duty of the president, who, at this time, was Andrew Jackson. Jackson,

President Andrew Jackson (1767-1845), nicknamed Old Hickory because of his toughness, repeatedly challenged Chief Justice Marshall and his Court decisions.

who admired neither Marshall nor Indians, refused to do anything. Encouraged by the president's inaction, other states challenged the federal government. This convinced Marshall that all his life's work had gone for nothing. "I yield slowly and reluctantly to the conviction that our Constitution cannot last," he wrote.

But the the states went too far even for President Jackson. When South Carolina declared its right to disregard any national law it did not like, Jackson realized that without enforcement of all federal laws, the nation would fall apart. After he ordered the states to obey federal laws or to prepare to fight, the states' rebellion against the Court died.

However, Jackson's action came too late to win back Marshall's trust. Although the chief justice longed to retire from the court and spend time with his family, he did not want Jackson to name his successor. So Marshall hung on to his position as chief justice in the hope that Jackson would be defeated in the next election. But Jackson was still in office when Marshall died of liver disease in 1835.

Marshall's legacy, however, was firmly in place. When he joined the Supreme Court, the states were so loosely organized and stubbornly independent that they could easily have become their own separate nations. Throughout his entire 34-year term, he swam against the tide of the majority who were suspicious of national government and wanted each state to be left alone to operate as its people saw fit. With an iron will shaped at Valley Forge, he built a framework under which the states could work and grow together into a strong nation. Marshall's role in almost single-handedly establishing the authority of the Supreme Court and the federal government has made him the symbol of American law.

John Adams (1735-1826), the second president of the United States, considered his nomination of John Marshall to the Supreme Court as his greatest contribution to the country.

John Adams, himself a president and patriot who could point with pride to his own accomplishments in helping to create the United States, best summed up the influence of John Marshall's Supreme Court. Near the end of his life, Adams declared, "My gift of John Marshall to the people of the United States was the proudest act of my life."

Despite many years of respected public service, one decision—Dred Scott—ruined the reputation of Chief Justice Roger Taney.

Chapter 2

Roger Taney:
The Dred Scott Villain

*H*ad Roger Taney (pronounced TAW nee) retired at the age of 79, he would be remembered by Americans as an able and even courageous public figure. Taney wisely steered the Supreme Court through the post-Marshall years. Contrary to the fears of Marshall supporters, Taney held on to most of the powers that Marshall had won for the Court. His moderate stand and calm guidance during his first 20 years as chief justice added to the Court's growing respect.

Unfortunately, the aging Taney destroyed his hard-won reputation with a single disastrous opinion. Many

Americans view the Dred Scott decision, authored by Taney in 1856, as the greatest blunder ever committed by the Supreme Court. The decision so badly split the country that, from the moment Taney read his opinion, a bloody war between the states could hardly be avoided.

The distrust and contempt provoked by the ruling crippled the Supreme Court's authority for several decades. The damage to Taney may well last throughout the history of the United States. Although legal experts rank Taney as one of the Supreme Court's greatest justices based on his overall record, he is primarily remembered by the public as the villain of the Dred Scott case.

Roger Brooke Taney was born on March 17, 1777, during the height of the American Revolution, to a prominent family in Calvert County, Maryland. He was raised on his parents' tobacco plantation, which was worked by black slaves.

According to tradition, family property passed to the eldest son. As the second of the Taney boys, Roger could not inherit the plantation and so his father groomed him for a career in law. Roger attended rural one-room schools and worked with private tutors until the age of 15. He then attended Dickinson College in Pennsylvania where, in 1795, he graduated with honors. For three years following graduation, he worked as an apprentice lawyer for a judge in Annapolis.

After being admitted to the bar in 1799, Taney tried to set up his own law practice in Annapolis. Finding the city overstocked with lawyers, however, he returned to Frederick, a town near his home. In 1799, Taney won a term in the Maryland state legislature as a Federalist. This was a poor time to be a member of the Federalist party. Jefferson's Democratic-Republicans had won the trust of the common people while the Federalists gained a reputation as the party of the wealthy, upper class. Unlike Marshall, the stately Taney looked and acted every bit the part of an upper-class gentleman, and in the election campaign, newspapers attacked his "aristocratic airs." He lost his bid for re-election in 1801, and his attempt to regain his seat in 1803 failed badly.

In 1806, Taney married Anne Key, whose brother, Francis Scott Key, later wrote "The Star-Spangled Banner." The Taneys were Roman Catholics and the Keys Episcopalians, and their mixed marriage was rather daring for their times. Roger and Anne compromised by agreeing to raise their sons as Catholics and their daughters as Episcopalians. Anne easily got the best of the arrangement, as the Taneys' six children were all girls!

Roger prospered as a lawyer and stayed active in the Federalist party until 1812. At that time, he split with the Federalists by favoring war with Great Britain. The Federalist party opposed the war, and they ridiculed the prowar Federalists as "Coodies." Taney was dubbed "King Coody."

Taney, however, got the last laugh. The antiwar

stance of the Federalists proved so unpopular with the voters that it ruined whatever influence the party had. As a war supporter, Taney was able to win election to the Maryland state senate in 1816. He served until 1821, by which time he had become an admirer of Andrew Jackson, a Democrat. Taney worked tirelessly for Jackson in the election of 1824 and helped him to win five of Maryland's 11 electoral votes in a losing cause.

Taney won election as Maryland's attorney general in 1827. He again directed Jackson's presidential campaign in Maryland in 1828. This time Jackson won and rewarded Taney for his efforts by naming him United States attorney general in 1831.

As attorney general, Taney stepped into a controversy when he alone among Jackson's cabinet members urged the president to veto a bill rechartering the Bank of the United States. Ever since a fraud scandal had turned up at the bank's Baltimore branch, Taney had been suspicious of the Bank of the United States. Jackson considered the recharter nothing more than a scheme to aid the rich. In 1833, he ordered Secretary of the Treasury Louis McLane to remove all federal government deposits from the Bank of the United States. McLane refused to take such radical action. Jackson then fired him and nominated Taney, a man he could trust, as his new secretary of the treasury.

While waiting for Congress to confirm his

appointment, Taney did as Jackson asked and withdrew the federal funds. Jackson's actions angered his opponents in Congress, and they rejected Taney's appointment. Jackson vowed to get revenge, and Taney returned to Maryland to wait for Jackson to make good on his promise.

The chance came in 1835 when Gabriel Duvall resigned from the Supreme Court. Jackson nominated Taney to fill the post. But again Congress turned down Taney's appointment on a close vote. Ten months later Jackson stubbornly put forward Taney a second time as his choice to replace the late Chief Justice Marshall. Again, Taney's nomination sparked the heated opposition of such respected statesmen as Daniel Webster, Henry Clay, and John Calhoun. They denounced Taney as a "political hack," unfit to be a judge. But a newly elected Congress, more friendly to Jackson, confirmed Taney in March of 1836 by a 29-15 vote.

Jackson's hostile attitude to the Marshall Court led many to fear that Taney would dismantle the Supreme Court. Following Taney's confirmation, Senator Daniel Webster wrote to a friend, "Judge Story thinks the Supreme Court is gone, and I think so, too."

To their surprise, the chief justice approached his new role thoughtfully and reasonably. Critics who had written him off as a radical firebrand found him instead to be a warm, honest, gentle person. Taney was far more sympathetic to states' rights than was Marshall, and not as favorable to corporations. However, the new chief justice made no sweeping changes in federal law. By softening some of Marshall's more extreme stances, Taney actually promoted better relations between the Court and members of Congress. Under Taney, the Supreme Court remained the nation's highest authority on questions of law. Henry Clay later admitted that his opposition to the chief justice's nomination had been a mistake.

The *Charles River Bridge Co. v. Warren Bridge Co.* case provided an example of the moderate tilt of the Taney Court toward the right state governments had to regulate private business. In 1785, the Massachusetts legislature granted the Charles River Bridge Company a charter to build a toll bridge over the Charles River in Boston. Then, in 1828, the legislature granted a charter to the Warren Bridge Company to build another toll bridge very near the original bridge.

Convinced that this new bridge would take away its business, the Charles River Bridge Company sued. Citing the *Dartmouth College v. Woodward* decision, they claimed that Massachusetts had no right to alter the charter arrangement by allowing another bridge. Taney's Court decided against the Charles River Bridge Company, yet it did not take the radical step of overruling the Dartmouth decision. Instead, the Court simply ruled that the original charter contained no promise

Three of the most powerful politicians of their day (top to bottom)—Daniel Webster (1782-1852) of Massachusetts, Henry Clay (1777-1852) of Kentucky, and John C. Calhoun (1782-1850) of South Carolina—vigorously opposed President Jackson and his nomination of Taney.

that the state would not grant charters to other competitors.

During Taney's first 20 years as chief justice, the Supreme Court quietly disposed of all matters. Most of these had to do with regulating commerce and resolving minor disputes between state and federal government. Sooner or later, though, the Court had to confront slavery—an issue that was dividing the nation. African slaves had been working for American masters ever since 1619. But in the early nineteenth century, a movement to abolish slavery grew in the northern states. The Missouri Compromise, passed by Congress in 1820, sought to strike a balance between increasingly hostile proslavery and antislavery forces. The compromise called for Missouri to enter the Union as a slave state while Maine entered as a free state in which slavery was banned. Further, the act banned slavery in the western territories that lay north of Missouri's southern border. With slave states and free states equally represented in Congress, the truce held for a while. Then the Union admitted California, Wisconsin, and Iowa as free states. Because this shifted the balance, the debate heated up again. This time, Illinois Senator Stephen Douglas tried to calm the waters with his Kansas-Nebraska Act. This law, passed in 1854, said that in the Kansas and Nebraska territories, the people could vote on the issue of slavery. The law angered antislavery forces because Nebraska, which had been set aside as a free state by the

Missouri Compromise, was now open to the possibility of slavery.

At about this time, the Dred Scott case made its way to the Supreme Court. Dred Scott was a slave owned by John Emerson, an army doctor stationed in Missouri. In 1834, Emerson took Scott with him when he was transferred to a post in Illinois. Since slavery was illegal in Illinois, Scott technically became a free man. While in the North with Emerson, he married and had children.

Both Emerson and Scott returned to Missouri in the

Stephen Douglas (1813-1861), who in 1858 would engage another Illinois politician, Abraham Lincoln, in a famous series of debates, worked tirelessly in the Senate to hold the country together.

late 1830s, where Scott was again considered a slave. When Emerson died in 1843, Scott and his family became the property of Emerson's widow. She moved to New York and married an abolitionist (an antislavery activist) and left Scott in the charge of Peter Blow in Missouri.

Blow disliked slavery and wanted to use Scott as a test case to force the courts to take a stand on the issue. So, in 1846, he urged Scott to sue for his freedom. A district court upheld Scott's appeal in 1850. On an appeal, however, the Missouri Supreme Court ruled that, regardless of his years of freedom in the North, Scott became a slave again as soon as he crossed the Missouri border.

Ownership of Scott was then passed from Blow to an abolitionist named Sanford, who helped Scott set up a test case in federal court. Because Scott was suing Sanford for his freedom, the case became known as *Scott v. Sandford* (misspelled in official records) even though both men were on the same side of the slavery issue. As the Supreme Court studied the case, both pro- and anti-slavery forces hoped for a favorable ruling.

Despite growing up on a plantation worked by slaves, Taney had given mixed signals on his own views toward slavery. He had long ago freed the slaves whom he had inherited, yet he strongly supported the rights of slave owners. As United States attorney general he had supported a South Carolina law that imprisoned all free blacks who worked on ships anchored in South Carolina ports. Yet he had supported a Pennsylvania law that declared any slave entering its ports to be free.

Three strong opinions governed Taney's actions on the issue: First, he believed that states held all powers of government except for those powers specifically given to the federal government by the Constitution. Second, he believed that law must respect the right of individuals to own property. Third, he regarded blacks as property rather than as people.

Taney's first instinct was to take the easy way out and avoid getting caught in the uproar. He agreed with a majority of the Court that wanted to dismiss the case without a hearing. These justices held that a slave was not a citizen and therefore could not bring a suit in federal court. But one Northern justice promised to present a passionate attack on slavery in his dissenting opinion. That prompted a Southern justice to write a strong proslavery opinion in support of the decision.

This convinced Taney that he could not avoid the issue. Knowing that a majority of the justices were from proslavery states and would join him in voting against Dred Scott, Taney agreed to argue the case. He blundered, however, when he decided to issue a broad ruling that he hoped would settle the explosive issue of slavery once and for all.

His own Court should have told him that a simple solution to the slavery issue was impossible. Although the Court ruled against Scott on a 7-2 vote, each of the nine justices issued separate opinions. In his opinion, Taney abandoned his usual caution and delivered a slashing assault on abolitionists. The chief justice stated that the writers of the Constitution "agreed that Negroes were beings of an inferior order" and were "so far inferior that they had no rights which the white man was bound to respect." He went on to declare the Missouri Compromise unconstitutional because it had taken away the property rights of individuals.

Taney had hoped to pour water on a burning issue so that the fire of antislavery would go away. However, he ended up pouring gasoline on the flames of the slavery controversy. The decision had little effect on Dred Scott, whose owners quickly gave him his freedom. But the ruling split the Democratic party. Southern Democrats pointed to the Court's ruling as proof that the territories could not abolish slavery and that the federal government had to protect slave holders in those territories. That interpretation of the decision alarmed Northern Democrats, who were already angered by Taney's fiery language. Some continued to support Douglas's plan of letting the territories decide for themselves whether to allow slavery. But many Northern Democrats, convinced that compromise on the slavery issue was hopeless, joined the new Republican party, which opposed slavery.

Republican candidate Abraham Lincoln then defeated the divided Democrats in the 1860 presidential elec-

Although former slave Dred Scott (1795-1858) would not live to see the Civil War, the Supreme Court decision in his case further split the country on the slavery issue and drove Americans closer to armed conflict.

tion. With emotions whipped into a frenzy by the controversy surrounding Dred Scott, the Southern states grew pale at the thought of a Lincoln presidency. They left the Union, and a year later the nation went to war.

Dred Scott proved a disaster both for the Supreme Court and for Taney. Losing the respect and confidence of the North, the Court drifted along for years without much authority. Newspapers and citizens so ridiculed Taney that even his proper and courageous acts drew scorn.

For example, in the early days of the war, John Merryman urged his fellow Marylanders to secede from the Union. President Lincoln believed that the Union could win the war only if the border states between the North and South, such as Maryland, stayed in the

Union. On his orders, Union forces arrested Merryman and locked him in a federal jail.

Merryman appealed to Taney to uphold his constitutional right as a private citizen to have his case heard in a civil court. Already reeling from the ridicule of much of the country, Taney must have known that challenging Lincoln would only invite further humiliation. Yet he bravely issued the order. Lincoln ignored it. Furious, Taney insisted that only Congress could suspend a citizen's right to a civil trial. But neither Taney nor the Court had enough importance at this time to override Lincoln.

The American public forgot the able leadership provided by Taney in his earlier years. Only much later, when historians sifted through the wreckage of Dred Scott, did people begin to value Taney again. According to one observer, "There was no sadder figure to be seen in Washington during the years of the Civil War" than Chief Justice Taney. Bearing the weight of his enormous error, he ended his days a tired, shriveled, lonely man and finally died on October 12, 1864, at the age of 87.

Under Taney the High Court fell so low in public esteem that President Lincoln (above) felt free to disregard the chief justice's orders.

*Fiercely opinionated Justice John Harlan spoke his mind—
or changed it—regardless of whether anyone else agreed
with him.*

Chapter 3

John Harlan: Last of the Tobacco-Spittin' Judges

*W*hen he spoke from the bench, Justice John Harlan could shake the courtroom like an ancient prophet proclaiming the anger of God. While other justices read from carefully prepared manuscripts, Harlan seldom consulted notes when he delivered his opinions. Eyes flashing as his voice thundered through the room, Harlan pounded the desk with his fist and shook his finger at opposing justices.

Harlan's stump-speaking style of justice had not impressed everyone. Long after Harlan's death, Justice

Felix Frankfurter dismissed him as "an eccentric exception" on the Court. On many of the important issues, Harlan stood by himself, opposed by all eight of his fellow Supreme Court justices. During his 34 years on the Court, Harlan wrote 316 dissenting, or disagreeing, opinions, more than all but five Supreme Court justices in history.

But time proved him correct on many of his most passionate stands. Harlan's predictions about the future of race relations in the country proved to be chillingly accurate. His courageous dissents established a foundation upon which the civil rights movement in America could later begin.

Ironically, this champion of equal rights for all was once a slave owner who agreed wholeheartedly with the Dred Scott decision. During the Civil War he threatened to lead his Union regiment over to the Confederate side if President Lincoln tried to free the slaves. He refused to free his own slaves until the law forced him to. At one time he actively campaigned for a political party that discriminated against Catholics and immigrants.

When Harlan began arguing for the doctrine of equal rights for all, his opponents ridiculed him for abandoning his principles. Harlan's response was typical of this no-nonsense, straight-talking Kentuckian, the man once described as "the last of the tobacco-spittin' judges": "Let it be said that I am right rather than consistent."

Fittingly, John Marshall Harlan was named after the revered chief justice who still presided over the Supreme Court when Harlan was born on June 1, 1833. The Harlans were one of the most respected families in Boyle County, Kentucky. When John was a toddler, his father won the first of two terms to the United States House of Representatives. As one of a group of conservative Democratic-Republicans known as Whigs, James Harlan later served as secretary of state and attorney general for Kentucky. Young John grew accustomed to seeing powerful national figures, such as Henry Clay, stopping by the Harlan mansion.

Because John was tutored at home through most of his childhood, he had time to go on frequent horseback rides with his father to political rallies. He enjoyed the political arena so much that he followed in his father's footsteps. After attending nearby Centre College, Harlan studied law at Transylvania University in Lexington, Kentucky. He passed his law exam in 1853, and he began practicing in his father's law office in Frankfort.

At that time, Harlan fell under the spell of the Native American party. "Americans should rule America" was their motto, and they meant only Americans who were like themselves. They distrusted all Roman Catholics and proposed that immigrants live in the United States for 21 years before being allowed to vote. Young Harlan proved to be a captivating speaker, and he helped his new party enjoy great popularity in Kentucky in the 1850s.

Unfortunately Harlan's style won more admiration for his party than votes for himself. Although he won a judgeship in Franklin County in 1858, he lost his race for United States Congress by 67 votes in 1859. By that time, the issue of slavery had broken the country in two.

Kentuckians were especially torn because so many of them had one leg in each camp. Most were as fiercely loyal to the Union as they were to the rights of slave owners, and the Harlans were no exception. They held no hatred toward African-Americans. Nothing could infuriate John's father like seeing a slave abused, and he had no qualms about representing free blacks in court. But John had been brought up to believe that slaves were better off under humane white masters than on their own. He argued the issue so persuasively that he even won Malvina Shanklin, the daughter of a Northern abolitionist, to his side. In 1856, John and Malvina married and went on to have six children.

During the 1860 presidential election, Harlan campaigned for the Constitutional Union party. This new party supported slavery but did not want the Southern states to secede from, or leave, the Union over the issue. John Bell, the party's presidential candidate, won the

Kentucky vote but lost the election to Abraham Lincoln.

When President Lincoln called for a volunteer army to fight against the rebellious Southern states, Harlan answered the call. Much as Harlan disliked Lincoln's policies, the United States was so important to him that he would go to war against his proslavery allies rather than see the Union destroyed. In 1861 he raised a thousand volunteers and formed the 10th Kentucky volunteers. Most of these were proslavery men attracted to his vow to make the regiment part of the Confederate army if Lincoln tried to abolish slavery.

Colonel Harlan's men were assigned to protect Kentucky from Confederate attack. The Confederates rarely challenged the Kentucky troops, and the only action Harlan saw was a brief skirmish or two with raiders. For him the war's biggest impact was to shake loose some of his prejudices. Harlan trained, marched, and fought alongside German immigrants, Catholics, and poor mountain boys. The effort, sacrifice, and loyalty that these people demonstrated made him ashamed of his previous narrow-minded views.

Harlan's military career was cut short when his father died in 1863. John Harlan immediately resigned his commission and campaigned to carry on his father's work in politics. In 1863 he was elected Kentucky's attorney general on a pro-Union platform. Yet he continued to oppose Lincoln's policies. When Lincoln

Near the Antietam, Maryland, battlefield in October 1862, President Lincoln (in stovepipe hat) faces General George B. McClellan, whom he would defeat in the presidential election of 1864. Army veteran Harlan, who opposed Lincoln's decision to free the slaves, backed McClellan in that election.

announced the Emancipation Proclamation, which freed the slaves of the Confederate states in 1863, Harlan protested that the blacks were private property, and he pronounced the act "null and void." In the 1864 presidential election, he voted for Lincoln's opponent.

When the war ended, Harlan was a politician in search of a party. The Whigs and the Constitutional Union parties had faded away. Many people in Kentucky hated the Republicans, who now controlled the federal government, because of their role in ending slavery. By default, angry Kentuckians flocked to the Democratic party. Like the Democrats, Harlan opposed civil rights legislation granting equal rights for African-Americans. But the white hatred unleashed against them in Kentucky following the Civil War appalled him. Mobs of whites terrorized blacks with whippings, burnings, and lynchings. When Harlan saw how Democratic officials ignored and even encouraged this brutality, he broke completely with his past.

Harlan joined the Republican party and lashed out at Democrats for letting racial hatred thrive in the state. He campaigned for "decency" and for equal rights for all. He defended a Black Methodist congregation against an attempt by the Southern Methodist Church to take over its property. Coming full circle on the slavery issue, he declared that slavery was "the most perfect despotism that ever existed on this earth." He spoke up for the interests of immigrants and Catholics, and he

61

promoted the radical idea of an income tax to finance education for those too poor to afford it.

In 1871, Harlan ran for governor of Kentucky as a Republican. Although Harlan argued his positions forcefully, he could not overcome the unpopularity of his party. His defeat in that election was followed by an even more decisive defeat in a nasty 1875 campaign for governor, which ended his involvement in state politics. Now Harlan focused his efforts on national politics. As a delegate to the Republican convention in 1876, he attempted to win the presidential nomination for his law partner, Benjamin Bristow. After six ballots, none of the candidates, least of all Bristow, showed any signs of gathering enough support to win the nomination. Realizing that Bristow had no chance to win, Harlan urged his fellow delegates from Kentucky to vote for his next best choice—Rutherford Hayes of Ohio. Harlan's support tipped the balance in favor of Hayes, who not only won the Republican nomination but the presidency.

Hayes returned this favor by nominating Harlan to the Supreme Court seat vacated by David Davis shortly after Hayes took office. Ironically, the main opposition to Harlan came from members of his own party who remembered Harlan's past and were not convinced he was a true Republican.

Harlan joined a Supreme Court that had not yet regained the respect it lost in the Dred Scott decision. Other branches of government and powerful business

Benjamin Bristow (1832-1896), Harlan's Republican ally in Kentucky and national politics, served as secretary of the treasury under President Ulysses S. Grant.

interests easily manipulated the Court. In the area of civil rights, the Court gradually chipped away at the protections granted to African-Americans at the end of the Civil War.

The civil rights cases of 1883 were the first important legal challenges that Harlan faced on the Court. These cases were a series of lawsuits filed against places that refused to serve blacks: theaters in New York City and San Francisco; a restaurant in Topeka, Kansas; a hotel in Jefferson City, Missouri; and a railroad in Tennessee. These refusals were in clear violation of the Civil Rights Act passed by Congress in 1873.

Eight of the nine justices rejected the lawsuits because they thought that the 1873 Civil Rights Act was unconstitutional. According to the majority, the Fourteenth Amendment, which guaranteed all citizens equal protection by the government, did not apply to the actions of private citizens. As an additional slap in the face, the Court said that the time had come to stop giving blacks "special favor of the law."

Harlan thought otherwise, and he thought the issue so important that he discarded his usual off-the-cuff manner of handing down an opinion. As the only voice speaking in favor of human freedom and dignity, he knew that his argument had to be powerful in order to be heard. He labored for weeks over his dissenting opinion, in which he would tell why he thought the majority of justices were wrong. Somehow, he could not find the words he wanted.

While Harlan was suffering from writer's block, his wife found an inkstand that had belonged to

Chief Justice Taney. The inkstand brought back memories of the Dred Scott decision, which Harlan now regretted deeply. Inspired by this memory, Harlan finished his brilliant dissent in which he declared, "Our Constitution is color blind and neither knows nor tolerates classes among its citizens."

Harlan's ringing dissent earned so many admirers that some citizens wanted to draft him to run for president. Meanwhile, the Court's decision encouraged segregation in many parts of the country, especially the South.

Harlan found himself alone in another case involving the Fourteenth Amendment. The state of California had put a man on trial without a grand jury indictment as required by the Constitution. In the *Hurtado v. California* case, only Harlan insisted that the Fourteenth Amendment overrode all state laws in guaranteeing the rights provided by the Constitution.

Harlan did not stand alone in the income tax debate, but again he was on the losing side. In 1894, Congress approved a plan to create an income tax in order to provide essential services to the poor. According to this new law, persons with incomes greater than $4,000 (a considerable amount at the time) would pay a tax rate of 2 per cent of their income. The Supreme Court was asked to decide if a tax on income was legal according to the Constitution.

By a 5-4 vote, the Court declared that the tax was

illegal. Condemning the tax as an "assault on thrift," the majority warned that such a tax would lead to "anarchy" and "class war." The Court ruled that the income tax was illegal because all taxes must be uniform. In other words, a person who made $1 million dollars a year could not be made to pay any more tax than someone who made $500 a year.

Harlan listened to these opinions with mounting fury. He glared at the majority judges and raised his eyebrows in mock disbelief. When his turn to speak came, he unleashed his fury on his fellow justices. "I regard this decision as a disaster!" he fumed. In his view, the Court was denying government the right to provide essential services. This decision, Harlan maintained, was another victory for the powerful. It placed the greatest burden of supporting the government on those who could least afford it. Eventually Americans came to agree with Harlan's opinion. In 1913, the country agreed to the Sixteenth Amendment, which legalized the graduated income tax.

Despite his court manner, Harlan was far from an obnoxious, ill-tempered loud complainer. In his dealings with others, he was courteous and well mannered. His sociable nature and sense of humor made him easy to be around. But when his colleagues insisted on blocking what he saw as the pathway to decency, Harlan breathed fire! He dissented when the Court said constitutional rights did not apply to the territories of the United

States in Puerto Rico, Hawaii, and the Philippine Islands. He dissented when the Court ruled that the laws protecting African-American voters from violence at the polls were illegal.

The one Harlan dissent that stands above the rest was his opinion in *Plessy v. Ferguson*. This case involved an 1890 Louisiana law that required railroads to provide separate passenger cars for whites and blacks. A group of civil rights advocates decided to challenge the law. With the support of the railroad company, which did not want the expense and hassle of providing separate cars, a test case was set up.

In June of 1892, Homer Plessy boarded a railroad car designated for whites and took his seat. Although Plessy was only one-eighth black, the conductor asked him to leave the coach. Plessy refused and was arrested. The court of New Orleans Judge John Ferguson convicted and fined Plessy. Plessy then appealed the decision to the Supreme Court.

Harlan again found himself alone on the side of equal rights for all. On May 18, 1896, the Supreme Court announced its 8-1 decision upholding the Louisiana law. The majority declared that "enforced separation of the two races does not mean unequal" and that "separate but equal" facilities did not violate equal protection rights under the law. They dismissed protests that the law humiliated or demeaned African-Americans. If they felt that the Louisiana law was insulting or labeled them as inferior, that was "solely because the colored race chooses to put that construction on it."

Harlan shredded the faulty logic of that opinion with his usual mixture of common sense and fiery oratory. He pointed out that the law obviously demeaned people of the "colored race" since its purpose was not to exclude whites from any coach but to exclude blacks from white coaches.

"What can more certainly arouse race hatred . . . than a state enactment which . . . proceeds on the ground that colored citizens are so inferior and degraded that they cannot be allowed to sit in public coaches occupied by white citizens," said Harlan. With a clear vision of the future, he warned that the court's ruling would result in "aggression, more or less brutal" against African-Americans.

Harlan's prediction proved accurate. The *Plessy v. Ferguson* decision sparked a rash of "Jim Crow" laws segregating the races. The "seeds of race hatred" that Harlan spoke of were planted, and race discrimination became a way of life, especially in the South. Southern states used Jim Crow laws to keep blacks in their place and to prevent them from enjoying equal rights under the law. "Separate but equal" proved to be anything but equal.

Shortly after the beginning of the 1911 Supreme Court term, John Marshall Harlan developed bronchitis. He died three days later at the age of 78. Nearly half a century would pass before the Supreme Court finally caught up to Harlan's understanding of equality before the law.

Tall and distinguished of bearing, with white hair and a big, bushy mustache, Justice Oliver Wendell Holmes, Jr., was among the most learned men of his time.

Chapter 4

Oliver Wendell Holmes: The Philosopher Judge

*P*resident Theodore Roosevelt was well satisfied with his choice of Oliver Wendell Holmes as associate justice of the Supreme Court in 1902. Holmes brought to the court 20 years of experience as associate justice and chief justice of the Massachusetts Supreme Court. Tall and erect, sporting his magnificent trademark moustache, Holmes presented a striking picture of authority. Most importantly, Roosevelt was sure he could count on Holmes to support the many reforms he was trying to make in the regulation of business.

Shortly after Holmes joined the Supreme Court, an

71

important case came up for consideration. Roosevelt's administration was trying to use a new law to break up the North Securities Company, a company that Roosevelt considered a dishonest tool of powerful railroad owners. The Supreme Court upheld the Roosevelt administration by the narrowest of margins. But to Roosevelt's dismay, one of the justices voting against him was Holmes. "I could carve out of a banana a judge with more backbone than that!" snapped Roosevelt.

Roosevelt totally misunderstood Holmes. Here was a man who had watched rank after rank of his friends shot to pieces in war and knew the feel of hot lead slamming into his throat. If Holmes had a problem with courage it was that he had too much, not too little. Holmes thrived on debate, argument, and controversy. He once commented that "I don't mind when the lads say I was wrong, it is when they say 'Mr. Justice Holmes was correct' that I find them insufferable." He enjoyed making outrageous comments to disturb the stagnant thinkers around him. Holmes did not merely question the endless pages of picky details necessary to document a case. Instead he growled, "I hate facts." Holmes assumed Harlan's role as the "Great Dissenter" of the Supreme Court. But whereas Harlan dissented, or disagreed, with the majority of the justices out of moral outrage, Holmes did so out of a burning curiosity that refused to accept commonly held beliefs without question. Beneath that stately, upper-class appearance beat the heart of a rebel. A tireless reader and an eager philosopher, Holmes dug more deeply into issues than the average judge. Because his conclusions unsettled his fellow justices, he could seldom persuade them to his way of thinking. But in the long run, Holmes greatly influenced the way Americans look at the law.

Oliver Wendell Holmes, Jr., was born on March 8, 1841, in Boston, Massachusetts. He carried with him a name that forever reminded him of his solid New England roots. His ancestors—the Olivers, the Wendells, and the Holmes—had all lived in Boston for two centuries. Oliver Wendell Holmes, Sr., enjoyed a wide reputation as a poet, physician, and intellectual.

The younger Holmes, known as Wendell throughout his childhood, was educated at the best schools in Boston, although he was never more than an average student. He resented living in the shadow of his famous father. Whether or not this contributed to his rebellious nature, Wendell preferred to learn things his own way. He spent much of his childhood with his nose in a book. The reading habit stayed with him all his life and left him with more than 14,000 books in his personal library.

Holmes attended Harvard University where he was named class poet. He wrote frequently about philosophical issues. "A hundred years ago we burnt men's bodies for not agreeing with our religious tenets; we still burn

Oliver Wendell Holmes, Sr. (1809-1894) passed on to his son the intellectual gifts that he himself used to practice medicine and write successful poetry and novels. The senior Holmes also taught anatomy and physiology at Dartmouth and at Harvard, where he became dean of the medical school in 1847.

their souls," he wrote in 1861. He had little interest, however, in trying to change society to suit his ideals. Holmes was late in joining the abolitionist movement that had swept Boston, and remained skeptical of reform efforts throughout his life.

Nonetheless, he answered President Lincoln's call

for soldiers to fight the Civil War against the South. For three years, Holmes stood in the front lines of one of the most horrifying events in American history. At the Battle of Ball's Bluff in northern Virginia, he was wounded and barely escaped with his life across a river riddled by Confederate fire. Almost a year later, in September of 1862, he took a bullet in the neck at the bloody battle of Antietam, and within a few months was shot in the foot at Fredericksburg.

After three years of this brutal fighting, a weary, frustrated Holmes resigned from the army. He returned to Boston a changed man. He had hardened himself against the terror and the suffering around him to do his job as a soldier. But he had paid a price for his bravery. Scarred by the loss of so many friends in battle, Holmes never again tried to develop close friendships. He rarely went out in public and was so secretive that he asked people to burn the letters he wrote to them. Holmes's philosophy of life centered on cold, detached analysis. He doubted others. Above all, he made fun of idealistic notions such as "rights" or "duties."

His father's poor opinion of the legal profession did not stop Wendell from attending Harvard Law School after he returned from the war. In 1867 in Boston, Holmes set up his law practice, which was helped by his many contacts among influential families. Throughout his life he searched for intellectual challenges beyond his regular case load. For example, he regularly met in the evenings with a small group of men to discuss philosophy.

Holmes, who could be something of a snob, was convinced that no one deserved to be called a scholar unless he had published a book by the age of 40. He began working towards this goal in his early thirties. His book, which was inspired by a series of lectures he had prepared for a law course, challenged standard thoughts about the nature of law. The task was so huge and the writing so strenuous that Holmes isolated himself while working on the book. For five years he spent his weekends and evenings writing, thinking, and studying, with his wife, Fanny, as his only companion. Holmes barely beat his self-imposed deadline, publishing *The Common Law* in 1881, just a few months before his fortieth birthday.

The Common Law upset legal tradition by arguing that the law is not an unchanging set of abstract principles as most scholars believed. Rather, Holmes described how law changes to respond to the changing conditions and needs of society. In one of his typically provoking statements, he wrote, "The life of the law has not been logic; it has been experience."

Holmes stated his case so brilliantly that he earned wide respect as a law scholar. Impressed, Harvard University hired him as a professor of law in 1882. But Holmes taught for less than a year before he was hit by "a stroke of lightning which changed the whole course" of his life. The governor of Massachusetts offered him the job of associate justice of the Massachusetts Supreme Court. Holmes accepted with enthusiasm, eager for the chance to "think under fire." For the next 20 years, his sharp mind and cleverness dominated the Massachusetts Court. Holmes, who was named chief justice of the court in 1899, proved exceptionally skillful in dealing with the mostly routine cases that came before him. Of the 1,290 opinions that he wrote for the court, only one was ever reversed by a higher court.

In his most daring opinion while on the Massachusetts Court, Holmes came out in favor of the rights of labor unions. He declared that a strike was "a lawful instrument in the universal struggle for life." Most of the older, established families of Boston regarded this as a betrayal, and Holmes made powerful enemies.

These enemies tried hard to deny Holmes a spot on the United States Supreme Court in 1902. Only an assassin's bullet brought Holmes the nomination. President William McKinley had promised the seat to someone else. But when McKinley was killed in office, the new president—Theodore Roosevelt—felt free to nominate his own judge. Upon hearing that Holmes was the choice, Senator George Hoar of Massachusetts tried to change Roosevelt's mind. "I have never heard of anybody speaking of Judge Holmes as an able judge," he

President Theodore Roosevelt (1858-1919) paid no heed to the many politicians who advised against his nomination of Holmes to the Court—but later had reason to wish he had listened to them.

insisted. Roosevelt stuck to his choice, though. The Senate confirmed Holmes on December 4, 1902.

Holmes offered no dissents during the first year and a half at this newest intellectual challenge. But gradually he made his presence felt. The Supreme Court at that time tended to favor wealthy business interests. The Court also took a dim view of lawmakers meddling with society. Holmes, however, believed that the law was flexible and could adapt to the changes in society. Further, he insisted that the Supreme Court had no business deciding whether a law was a good idea or a poor one. The elected officials of Congress and the state legislatures could debate the wisdom of their laws. The Court's role was to make sure the laws abided by the Constitution. "There is no constitutional prohibition against legislators making fools of themselves," he insisted.

Holmes repeatedly disagreed with the Court's restrictions against legislatures. In 1908 the Supreme Court ruled as unconstitutional a congressional law requiring that a railroad company pay compensation to any worker maimed or killed because of the company's neglect. Holmes voted to uphold the law. In 1918 Congress tried to stop employers from taking advantage of children, so it passed a law forbidding the interstate (between states) shipment of products made in factories that employed children. The Supreme Court also ruled this law unconstitutional. Once again, Holmes disagreed.

This pattern continued throughout his years on the Court. The 1921 case of *Truax v. Corrigan* involved an Arizona law that barred state courts from stopping a labor dispute except in extreme cases. By the narrowest of margins, the Supreme Court shot down the law as an invasion of property rights. Speaking for the minority opinion, Holmes argued, "I can feel no doubt of the power of legislation to deny" the courts the power to stop strikes. He reminded his colleagues that judges ought to be more careful about striking down laws just because the laws disagreed with their "own concept of public policy." Later in life he put the issue even more bluntly. "About 75 years ago, I learned that I was not God," he said.

Holmes fought this same battle in several other Supreme Court cases involving labor union activities. When lawmakers said that railroad companies could not fire workers for joining a union, the Court rejected the law. Holmes dissented. When the Court ruled that state legislatures did not have the power to protect a worker's right to join a union, Holmes again argued that the judges were overstepping their bounds and explained, "Whether in the long run it is wise for the working men to enact legislation of this sort is not my concern, but I am strongly of the opinion that there is nothing in the Constitution of the United States to prevent it."

Holmes again took his colleagues to task in the *Adkins v. Children's Hospital* case of 1923. There the court ruled that a law creating a minimum wage for women was illegal. Arguing for the flexibility of law,

Holmes stated that if experts in such matters thought this law a good course of action for society, then it ought to stand.

Holmes's opinions were generally more understandable and far more memorable than those of his colleagues. He was not one to soften his opinions by using diplomatic phrases, and he had no patience for overblown legal jargon. He put his points simply and clearly in descriptive language seasoned with a touch of wit.

The most memorable of his opinions were those attempting to define the line between individual rights and the rights of society. His thinking on this issue demonstrated his struggle with the flexibility of the law. Holmes hated the notion of absolute ideas—those that were considered true for all time and in all cases. As a result, he tried to fashion flexible guidelines in deciding cases about individual rights. *Schenck v. United States* was such a case.

Charles Schenck believed that the practice of drafting young men into military services violated their constitutional rights. During World War I, he wrote a pamphlet in which he urged Americans to resist the draft. The government arrested, tried, and convicted Schenck of violating the Sedition Act of 1918. Believing that the Bill of Rights guaranteed him the right to present his pamphlet, Schenck appealed to the Supreme Court.

In his most famous majority decision, Holmes upheld Schenck's conviction. Freedom of speech, according to Holmes, did not grant the right to say anything. For example, it did not give one the right to "shout 'fire' in a crowded theater." The question was where one drew the line between a person's right to an opinion and society's right to maintain order.

Holmes argued that this line had to be flexible. "The character of every act depends upon the circumstance in which it is done," he maintained. Holmes thought that a good test to decide such cases would be "whether the words are used in such circumstance and are of such a nature as to create a clear and present danger" to the country. Holmes decided that Schenck's words would not have presented a danger had they been written in peace time. But since the country was at war, the pamphlet presented a danger that the government could suppress.

When the Supreme Court began applying the "clear and present danger" too rigidly, though, Holmes saw that he had not found the perfect solution to the question of individual rights versus society's rights. Prodded by his friend, Justice Brandeis, Holmes began leaning more in favor of individual rights.

The case of *Abrams v. United States* sought to apply the 1918 Sedition Act against five Russian immigrants. The government arrested and convicted these immigrants for urging workers in the military weapons industry to go on strike to protest the involvement of the United States in the Russian Revolution. The

Supreme Court, using Holmes's standard, upheld the conviction.

But Holmes, believing that the Court was using his standard as a general tool to stop the freedom of expression, dissented. Holmes admitted that people naturally try to squash ideas they think false or dangerous. "But when men have realized that time has upset many fighting faiths, they may come to believe, even more than they believe the very foundations of their own conduct, that the ultimate good desired is better reached by free trade of ideas—that the best test of truth is the power of the thought to get itself accepted in the competition of the market."

Holmes went yet a step further in voting to overrule the conviction of Benjamin Gitlow in 1925. Rejecting the idea that the Bill of Rights does not protect free speech if it is "an incitement" to disorder, Holmes declared that "every idea is an incitement." He insisted that only in extreme cases was the government justified in preventing the free exchange of ideas.

Throughout his career, Holmes argued that judges should keep their own personal beliefs out of legal decisions. Yet even he occasionally allowed his own standards of behavior to peek through. In 1928 the Supreme Court ruled that the government could use wiretapping to gather evidence against criminals. But the idea of the government resorting to a "criminal activity" to catch criminals offended his notion of civilization. "I think it a

A member of the American Communist party, Benjamin Gitlow spent three years in New York's Sing Sing Prison for his political views. Based on Gitlow's constitutional right to free speech, however, Justice Holmes argued that the conviction should not have stood.

lesser evil that some criminals should escape than that the government should play an ignoble part," he said.

Even as he approached the age of 90, Justice Holmes displayed a gift for quickly cutting through to the core of a debate. He went out of his way to compliment young lawyers who impressed him with their argument. But he had little patience for those who strayed from their points. Many lawyers arguing in front of the Court believed that Holmes was taking notes of their remarks, when in fact he had lost patience with them and was writing personal letters.

Holmes so enjoyed the challenge of legal questions that he stayed on the Court until January 12, 1932. By that time his wit and personality had made him one of the more popular folk heroes in the country. "America's most respected man of law," as Holmes was labeled, lived three more years before meeting his death on March 6, 1935, at the age of 93.

As a lawyer engaged in private practice for nearly 40 years, Louis Brandeis represented business owners and workers alike. He believed that treating workers fairly served the economic interests of both employers and employees—an idea that many business owners of the early 1900s disliked.

Chapter 5

Louis Brandeis:
The People's Lawyer

*L*ouis Brandeis traveled a road to the Supreme Court that was entirely different from his fellow Boston lawyer Oliver Wendell Holmes, Jr. Whereas Holmes descended from a long, established line of American Protestants, Brandeis came from a family of Jewish immigrants. While Holmes wrapped his life in a cocoon of philosophy and legal history, Brandeis made his mark in practical business law.

Holmes disliked reform movements; Brandeis involved himself in almost every social cause that came along. Holmes, the war-scarred Civil War veteran, projected a coolness that held people at arm's length. Emotions and personal sympathy played almost no part in his life. Brandeis's laser-bright eyes projected the intensity of his personality. He so involved himself with social injustice and the sufferings of the common people that he became known as "The People's Lawyer." Holmes thought facts could be too easily manipulated; he preferred to rely on reasoning, logic, and experience. Brandeis came to the Court armed with an avalanche of data to support his views. Holmes had little time for notions of morality, spirituality, and eternal truth. Brandeis believed firmly in all three.

Yet Brandeis joined forces with his opposite to reform a Supreme Court bound by tradition and close ties with powerful business interests. Holmes staked out his positions indifferent to whether anyone agreed with him. Joining Holmes on the Court, Brandeis brought with him the gift of relentless persuasion. Brandeis's skill as a problem solver and a businessman made him an effective force in finding legal solutions for social problems. Virtually all lawyers adopted his style of presentation, the Brandeis brief, as the model for arguing cases before the Supreme Court.

Brandeis's parents, Adolph and Fredericka, fled their comfortable, middle-class life in Bohemia during a period of civil unrest in 1848. They settled in Louisville, Kentucky, together with several others in their extended family. Louis David Brandeis, the youngest of their four children, was born in Louisville on November 13, 1856.

With the Civil War fast approaching, Louis grew up in exactly the kind of conflict-filled environment his family had hoped to escape. His most vivid childhood memories were of blue-coated soldiers camped near his home—reminders of the war in progress. The Brandeises also came under criticism from their neighbors for their firm antislavery stance.

Fortunately for them, the citizens of Kentucky remained pro-Union despite their views on slavery, and the border state was spared any major battles. As a supplier of grain and produce, Adolph Brandeis turned a brisk business filling contracts to feed the Union army.

While the war raged, Louis found refuge in books. He learned easily and handled a heavy load of advanced courses in school with no problem. Despite his early mastery of his studies, however, he had no confidence when making the type of oral presentations at which he would later excel. As the top student at his Louisville high school, Brandeis was scheduled to give a speech at a school program. Numb with terror at the prospect, Brandeis was overjoyed to come down with a case of laryngitis just in time to avoid the speech.

As a teen, Brandeis changed his middle name to "Dembitz" in honor of his uncle, Lewis Dembitz. Brandeis idolized Uncle Lewis—a scholarly, religious lawyer whom Brandeis called a "living university."

Fifteen-year-old Louis Brandeis earned top grades in almost every subject, as his 1871-1872 report card shows. According to his high school's grading system, 1 was "very bad;" 2 was "bad;" 3 was "indifferent;" 4 was "good;" 5 was "excellent;" and 6 was "without fault."

Brandeis not only followed his uncle's career path as a lawyer, but gained from him an interest in religious traditions that his own parents had ignored.

In 1872, Adolph Brandeis could see that a business recession was coming. He decided to ride out the bad times in Europe, where his children could gain some insight into their family roots. Although Adolph returned to the United States in 1873, Louis remained in Europe for three years, studying at German schools and under private tutors.

The homesick nineteen year old finally returned to the United States in 1875 and immediately enrolled at Harvard Law School in Massachusetts. Although two years younger than the rest of his class, he had no trouble keeping up with the other students. Brandeis graduated in 1878 and attempted to start a law office in St. Louis, but he returned to Massachusetts after a few months. That year he met Oliver Wendell Holmes, Jr., with whom he began to spend evenings discussing legal and philosophical issues.

As a lawyer, Brandeis combined a sharp business sense with his love of learning. He made good money at his practice and invested his earnings shrewdly. He and his wife, Alice, whom he had married in 1891, lived simply and kept themselves under a strict budget. This formula made them extremely wealthy.

At the same time, Brandeis began to view his law office as a laboratory for social research. As a business lawyer, he was most concerned with economic issues. Whenever he took a case, Brandeis did an exhaustive search to discover all the angles of the situation. Easily slicing through the maze of figures and accounting procedures that baffled most citizens, he uncovered a host of dishonest dealings. Frequently, Brandeis discovered facts that disturbed him. In the 1880s, for example, he exposed the heavy influence of the liquor industry on corrupt Massachusetts legislators. Later, he found an even bigger nest of corruption in the life insurance industry.

His findings gave him a dark view of society. When his daughter complained about some small injustice in her life, he told her, "If you will just start with the idea that this is a hard world, it will be that much simpler."

But no matter how great the problem, Brandeis did not shrug his shoulders in despair. He almost always took an active role in solving whatever injustice he uncovered. He spent more and more time working without fees for civic reform and spent less time on his regular practice. Among the causes Brandeis fought for were labor unions, women's rights, civil liberties, programs to provide assistance for the poor, and fair government regulation of industries. Brandeis also became attracted to Zionism, which promoted the creation of the Jewish state of Israel. Eventually he became a world leader in that movement. Yet even with his highly disciplined budgeting of time, all this work cut into his family time and left him without much of a social life.

Theodor Herzl (1860 -1904) was the father of modern Zionism, an international movement that led to the establishment of Israel in 1948. Justice Brandeis, an American Zionist leader, who in 1919 visited Palestine (as Israel was then called), wrote that his work for Zionism was "on the whole, the most worthwhile of all I have attempted."

Brandeis became especially concerned with the shameless amounts of money amassed by some clever, ruthless operators of giant corporations. He saw how certain financial interests had the power to manipulate the entire economy. Declaring "bigness" a curse that helped a select few to push around ordinary people,

Brandeis set off as a lone knight taking on some of the most powerful dragons in business. He waged campaigns against such giants as railroads, transportation and insurance companies, banks, and utilities.

Brandeis was able to battle these giants on an equal footing because of his genius at solving problems and presenting facts. When he fought a proposed railroad increase, he did not simply complain about how this would hurt small businesses. Brandeis pored over large quantities of figures and then demonstrated in court how the railroad could save millions of dollars without a rate increase. Not even those who knew Brandeis expected he could win the *Muller v. Oregon* case, which reached the Supreme Court in 1908. This dispute concerned a challenge to an Oregon state law. The law said that women employees could work a maximum of ten hours per day. Although the Oregon law sounds sexist today, it was an attempt to protect women from abusive employers. The Supreme Court had declared unconstitutional other attempts by state and federal legislatures to pass laws regulating business conditions.

Arguing the case for the state of Oregon, Brandeis introduced what came to be known as the "Brandeis brief." This consisted of a short summary of the important points of his case, followed by many pages of data in support of his points. His flawlessly documented argument showing the benefits of the law so impressed the Court that it voted to uphold the Oregon statute.

Although Brandeis earned the respect from lawyers and the admiration of the common people for his work, he also made powerful enemies who felt threatened by him. One observer called Brandeis "the most liked and the most hated man at the Bar in America." In 1909 "The People's Lawyer" added the president, William Howard Taft, to his list of foes. Brandeis plowed through a web of government statements and figures to show that Taft's Department of the Interior was lying about the sale of some public land.

Brandeis's work captured the respect of Woodrow Wilson, the Democrat who ran against Taft in the 1912 election. Wilson asked Brandeis to be one of his key advisors. When he captured the presidency, Wilson wanted to name Brandeis as his attorney general. After heated protests from Brandeis's enemies in Boston's legal community, however, Wilson backed off. He continued to rely on Brandeis for advice and looked for another opportunity to use the man's talents.

In 1916 Wilson saw his chance and touched off one of the most bitter debates in the history of Supreme Court confirmations by selecting Brandeis. Brandeis's enemies massed against him. The American Bar Association, former President Taft, the president of Harvard University, and more than 50 Boston attorneys declared that Brandeis was "not fit" for the Supreme Court. This time Wilson held firm. Brandeis was eventually confirmed by a vote of 47 to 22, with 27 senators not voting.

The 1924 Supreme Court. Standing, from left, are: Pierce Butler, Louis Brandeis, George Sutherland, and Edward Sanford. Seated, from left, are: Willis Van Devanter, Joseph McKenna, William Howard Taft (chief justice), Oliver Wendell Holmes, and James McReynolds.

Prejudice had stirred some people to oppose a Jewish justice. Supreme Court Justice James Clark McReynolds provided the most obnoxious evidence of bigotry. For three years McReynolds refused to speak to Brandeis, and even eight years later, he refused to sit next to Brandeis in the Court's 1924 group photograph.

But the bulk of the opposition to Brandeis simply feared that he was a radical who was out to stir up a revolution against the American free enterprise system.

These fears did not prove true. As one who had profited by the free enterprise system, Brandeis strongly supported it. His goal in trying to "curb the excesses of capitalism" that put so much wealth and power in the hands of a few was to prevent social unrest that this unfairness provoked.

Further, Brandeis shared the opinion of Justice Holmes that judges should not impose their political and personal views on the law. Although Holmes thought his colleague occasionally slipped into his old role as "The People's Lawyer," Brandeis generally resisted the urge to legislate from the bench. Altogether, the "radical" Brandeis voted with the majority on more than 80 percent of the cases that came before him.

Brandeis's strong suit as a judge was facts and figures rather than words. His written opinions could be as long and complicated as those of Holmes were short and to the point. Holmes often despaired of reading his friend's heavily footnoted presentations. Yet Brandeis had a command of information that provided him with the force of practical persuasion that Holmes lacked. When the two joined forces, they became a tough team to beat.

Like Holmes, Brandeis believed that the Court needed to recognize that society was continually changing. As a master problem solver, he had no patience with a Court that refused to give lawmakers the flexibility to find new solutions to a new generation of problems.

Brandeis argued that "government is not an exact science." He believed that "a courageous state may choose to serve as a laboratory" to test new methods of dealing with problems, and he repeatedly pleaded with his colleagues not to "close the door to experiment within the law."

As their terms on the Supreme Court overlapped by 15 years, Brandeis voted in many of the same cases as Holmes and usually came down on the same side. In the *Truax v. Corrigan* case, in which the Court supported a suit by restaurant owners to stop employees from picketing, Brandeis dissented. Arguing against the Court's traditional, unbudging support in favor of property owners, Brandeis said that the conflict showed how the "rights of property and the liberty of the individual must be remolded from time to time."

Brandeis was so committed to active problem solving that this "People's Lawyer" came down on the side of big business when he saw it attempt to respond to the changing times. The Court ruled that an association in which lumber companies joined together to share information on production, stock, and sales violated the antitrust laws. Brandeis, however, dissented, for he believed that competitors had to exchange information and to regulate their production in response to that information. He saw this as nothing more than "substituting knowledge for ignorance."

During his career as a lawyer, Brandeis never shied

Brandeis (right) with Holmes (center) and Justice Harlan F. Stone (1872-1946). Stone served on the Court with Brandeis for 14 years and often agreed with his dissenting opinions.

away from a fight and boldly attacked problems that needed solving. As a Supreme Court justice, he constantly encouraged his associates to show the same kind of adventurous spirit rather than to cling timidly to the safe and secure past. This attitude applied not only to the idea of lawmaking experiments but to experimentation with new ideas.

Surpassing Holmes as a champion of free speech, Brandeis wrote, "Those who won our independence by revolution were not cowards. They did not fear political change. They did not exalt order at the cost of liberty."

At the same time, Brandeis knew that taking a bold stand without command of the facts was reckless. In his dissent against the Court's approval of government wiretapping, Brandeis wrote, "The greatest dangers to liberty lurk in insidious encroachments by men of zeal, well-meaning but without understanding."

The best way to make certain that a government of the people acted both boldly and wise, Brandeis believed, was with "the power of reason as applied through public discussion." If people felt threatened by false or dangerous ideas, "the remedy to be applied" was "more speech, not enforced silence."

As a judge, Brandeis showed the strong sense of fairness that had moved him to get involved in social causes. When a self-serving Supreme Court ruled that federal judges were not bound to pay federal taxes, Brandeis and Holmes paid their taxes anyway. In the mid-1930s, Brandeis actively fought against President Franklin Roosevelt's attempt to get control of the Court by adding five new justices.

Brandeis continued to serve on the Supreme Court for seven years following the retirement of Holmes. He resigned from the Court on February 13, 1939, at the age of 82, and died of a heart attack on October 5, 1941.

Unlike Holmes, Brandeis stayed on the Court long enough to see his views accepted by the majority. By the time Brandeis resigned from the Court, most Americans and the majority of his fellow justices had come to agree with his approach to government: that legislators should be given a reasonable chance to solve social and economic problems that placed a heavy burden on the people.

*Pictured here as governor of New York, Charles Evans
Hughes successfully combined a political and judicial career
that spanned nearly four decades.*

Chapter 6

Charles Evans Hughes:
The Chief Umpire

*F*ew remarks made by Charles Evans Hughes have received as much attention as his comment that "we are under a Constitution, but the Constitution is what the judges say it is." Coming from a Supreme Court chief justice, the statement sounds rather arrogant and power-hungry.

But in fact, Hughes was not speaking of himself. He made the remark while governor of New York, well before he ever donned a judge's robe. Hughes believed the role of judges to be crucial in society, and as an avid baseball fan, he compared the role to that of an umpire in a baseball game. Umpires made the game run smoothly. They settled disputes quickly, kept a watchful eye for any cheating, and made sure the teams behaved properly.

The system worked only because each side agreed to abide by every decision, right or wrong, like it or not. Hughes loved to tell the story of the baseball umpire who was asked, whether a pitch was a ball or a strike. "It's nothing until I call it, and what I call it, it is!" barked the umpire. Hughes's remark about the Constitution was just a variation of the umpire's statement. It reflected Hughes's belief that "we secure our peace and confidence by loyal acceptance of the decisions of our umpires." Hughes believed that judges need the same type of unquestioned authority as umpires so that they can perform their roles as "the safeguard of our liberty and property."

As chief justice, Hughes faced a challenge to the Supreme Court's authority from the most powerful man in the United States, President Franklin Roosevelt. Hughes held his ground against Roosevelt's attempt to pack the Supreme Court with his own supporters. Thus the chief justice maintained the role of the Court as America's final arbiter, or umpire.

Hughes was born on April 11, 1862, to a school teacher and a Baptist minister in Glens Falls, New York.

His parents, who had no other children, showered attention and instruction on young Charles. At an age when most small children are exploring their world through play, Charles was drilled relentlessly on moral and academic lessons.

Charles was an astoundingly bright child who eagerly lapped up his parents' instruction. When he was sent to school at the age of six, he found that he had progressed far beyond his classmates. After enduring three weeks of boredom, he begged to continue studying at home. The curriculum and study schedule that the youngster prepared so impressed his parents that they agreed. Pushed hard by his parents, Charles continued his rapid pace of learning. By the age of eight he was reading the New Testament in the original Greek.

At the age of 11, Charles moved to New York City with his parents and there attended public school. Within a few years, he had mastered everything the schools could teach him. In 1876, the fourteen year old headed off to Madison College (now Colgate University) with the intention of studying for the ministry. Two years later he transferred to Brown University in Providence, Rhode Island. His parents, fearful that a roommate might be a bad moral influence on him, advised him to room by himself.

While at Brown the sixteen year old's deadly serious outlook began to thaw. The boy, who had never really been allowed any fun in his life, became fascinated with baseball. He realized that the minister's life for which his father had prepared him ever since Charles could talk was not for him. In December of 1880 he wrote his parents what must have been a difficult letter. In it he told them that he "felt no call" to the ministry. Instead, he planned to pursue a legal career.

With no money for law school following graduation from Brown, the nineteen year old took a job teaching Greek, Latin, and mathematics at a school in Delhi, New York. By 1882 his father had accepted Charles's career choice well enough that he agreed to help finance his continuing education. Charles studied law at Columbia Law School. Not only did he graduate with highest honors in 1884, he also achieved a near perfect score on his bar exam. By the age of 22, Hughes was well on his way to a promising career in law.

For the next 20 years, this extraordinarily talented man pulled back the throttle and settled down to a fairly routine, comfortable life. He married Antoinette Carter, the daughter of a law partner, in 1888. He taught at Cornell University Law School for a couple of years, then returned to his private practice. During those two decades, he accomplished nothing more daring than growing a beard that would be his trademark in an era of clean-shaven public servants.

This all changed when Hughes was appointed legal

advisor to a New York state legislative committee that was studying the way gas and utility rates were set. Hughes brought to the committee's attention the fact that the utility company was charging the government of New York City three times as much as private customers for this energy. Hughes's work so impressed another legislative committee investigating an insurance scandal that they hired him that same year. Again, Hughes discovered some alarming practices that led to reforms in the industry. With both Brandeis and Hughes on their side in the legal arena, consumers had a bright future in the northeastern United States.

Hughes's performance caught the attention of another active reformer, President Theodore Roosevelt. With the president's backing, Hughes ran for governor of New York on the Republican ticket in 1906. Hughes's reputation for integrity and efficiency carried him against the election tide. He was the only Republican candidate elected to a state office that year.

In two terms as governor, Hughes made good on his promise of providing "decent" government. Under his guidance, New York State took the national lead in actively working to cure social ills. Hughes supported innovations such as child labor laws and a commission to set utility rates. At the same time, he tried to control the cost of government, and he opposed the idea of a federal income tax.

A determined campaigner for his fellow Republicans, Hughes addresses a rural Minnesota audience on behalf of William Howard Taft, who would later win the 1908 presidential election.

Hughes's impressive record and growing popularity caused Republican presidential hopefuls to fear him as a rival. Some speculated that one reason that President Taft nominated him as a Supreme Court justice in 1910 was to eliminate him as a rival.

Hughes worked hard during his noncontroversial years as an associate justice and penned more opinions than any of his colleagues. Except for an occasional dissent from Holmes, these opinions were generally for a unanimous Court. The most important of these was a 1911 dispute over whether intrastate railroad companies (those operating strictly within a state) could charge cheaper rates than interstate railroad companies (those that crossed state borders) when their routes overlapped. The Court ruled they could not, because this interfered with interstate commerce. The ruling allowed Congress to construct an efficient national system of transportation.

The case of *McCabe v. Atchison, Topeka & Santa Fe Railroad* in 1914 provided an exception to the solidarity of the Court. Speaking for a narrow majority, Hughes ruled that railroads could not provide sleeping and dining cars for whites unless they also provided equal facilities for blacks.

To the dismay of his political rivals, not even the prestige of being a Supreme Court justice could shield Hughes from the temptation of presidential politics. In 1916 he resigned from the Court and captured the Republican nomination for president. Unfortunately, Hughes's normal, decent, high-minded standards got lost in the cutthroat environment of a national election. He ran a largely negative campaign against President Woodrow Wilson. Wilson, for his part, campaigned as the man who "kept us out of war" when, in fact, he was only a few months away from leading the United States into World War I.

Despite his campaign problems, Hughes was encouraged by the early results on election night. He went to bed convinced that he had been elected president. Morning brought the rude shock that Wilson had come out ahead.

Hughes went back to practicing law, but he kept a sharp eye on the political scene. In 1920 the New York State legislature refused to seat five Socialists who had won election to that body. Although personally opposed to socialism, Hughes wrote to the speaker of the house to argue that in a democracy, citizens and the government had to respect the people's choice. The speaker, however, ignored his advice.

In 1921 President Warren Harding called Hughes back to national affairs by naming him secretary of state. A woefully weak president, Harding was only too happy to give Hughes freedom to conduct foreign policy. With the world still reeling from the devastation of world war, Hughes tried to extend an open hand to other countries. He led an international movement to reduce the tensions and arms buildup that brought about the war. After resigning in 1925, he put his foreign relations expertise to use by going into the practice of international law.

Upon the resignation of Hughes's old rival, William

William Howard Taft (1857-1930) served as president of the United States from 1909 to 1913. Later, as the tenth chief justice of the Supreme Court (1921-1930), he often locked horns with Brandeis and, to a lesser extent, Holmes.

Howard Taft, as chief justice in 1930, President Herbert Hoover asked Hughes if he would consider taking over the spot. Hughes agreed only after the president and congressional leaders assured him that his nomination would cause no controversy.

They were wrong. Many politicians did not like the idea of a wealthy man, as Hughes had become, joining the Court at a time when the country was suffering from an economic depression. One senator charged that "no man so exemplifies the influence of powerful combinations in the political and financial world" as

Publisher of The Saturday Press, *Jay Near persistently tested the constitutional limits on freedom of the press with his outrageous headlines, scandalous stories, and abusive attacks on public officials.*

112

Hughes. Others could not forgive Hughes for abandoning the Court in 1916 to further his own political ambitions. The Senate Judiciary Committee voted against his confirmation. After an extended debate, the Senate finally confirmed Hughes by a 52 to 26 vote.

Hughes's term as chief justice proved to be as stormy as his first term on the Court was calm. One of the most sensational cases was *Near v. Minnesota*, decided by the court in 1931. Jay Near was the publisher of *The Saturday Press*, a Minneapolis newspaper that routinely printed reckless charges against public officials, often in insulting language. Public officials finally stepped in when *The Saturday Press* ran a series of articles charging that Jewish gangsters and corrupt police controlled Minneapolis. Near was convicted under a Minnesota law that banned that type of irresponsible accusation.

Hughes made no secret of his contempt for Near's newspaper. At the same time he believed that a ruling in favor of the Minnesota law would erode the freedom of the press—one of the very foundations of a free democracy. Hughes spoke for the majority in rejecting the Minnesota law. "The fact that the liberty of the press may be abused by miscreant purveyors of scandal does not make any the less necessary the immunity of the press from previous restraints in dealing with official misconduct."

The Court also stepped into a hornets' nest in the case of *United States v. MacIntosh* that same year. Hughes dissented from the majority view that the government could deny citizenship to those applicants who refused to promise to bear arms in defense of the country.

By far the greatest challenge facing Chief Justice Hughes was defining the limits of government power. With the Great Depression showing no signs of relaxing its grip, desperate people turned to the government for help. As the government began to assume more powers, the Court had to rule whether these new powers were allowed by the Constitution.

Much of the Court was still suspicious of Brandeis's argument in favor of legislative experiments. But out of sheer compassion for struggling citizens, the justices occasionally softened their stand. For example, the Supreme Court traditionally took a dim view of states interfering with legal contracts. But in 1934, the Court upheld a Minnesota law that allowed state courts to protect farmers from foreclosure. Hughes, speaking for the majority, justified the decision by saying that while a state could not cancel a contract, it could delay it.

The Court, however, was not ready to endorse the sweeping social changes engineered by President Franklin Roosevelt following his election in 1932. As part of his "New Deal" to put the United States back on its feet, Roosevelt introduced programs such as the National Industrial Recovery Act. This act attempted to stabilize the economy by introducing codes to regulate wages and

Chief Justice Hughes faced his greatest challenge from the White House when President Franklin Roosevelt repeatedly tried to sidestep the Court's authority in New Deal legislation.

working conditions in various industries. Trade associations made up of industry members, not the government, drew up these codes. Although Congress passed this grand scheme, the Supreme Court shot it down in 1936. In a unanimous decision, the Court ruled that the National Industrial Recoveries Act was unconstitutional

Former dean of the Columbia University Law School and attorney general under U.S. President Calvin Coolidge, liberal-minded Justice Harlan Stone succeeded Hughes as chief justice in 1941.

because it gave legislative, or law-making, power to an outside agency. In 1937 the Court also ruled against a New Deal law designed to stabilize the coal industry.

Roosevelt was furious. He blasted the Court as "nine old men" standing in the way of progress, and he rallied public opinion to his side. The president then proposed a plan that would allow him to appoint an extra judge for each justice over the age of 70. The makeup of the court in 1937 meant that he could appoint six new Supreme Court judges. According to Roosevelt, this would ease the heavy work load that was weighing down the Court.

Hughes knew that Roosevelt's real purpose was to bend the Court to his will. If this were allowed, the integrity of the Supreme Court would be in danger. The chief justice responded by gathering evidence to prove that the Supreme Court was not overworked. His argument laid bare the fact that Roosevelt was trying to pack

At a formal dinner in 1938, Chief Justice Hughes (left) chats with Vice-President John Nance Garner (1868-1967) and Justice Pierce Butler (1866-1939).

the Court. Congress and public opinion turned against Roosevelt, and the president scrapped his plan.

The chief justice then eased tensions with the president by taking a more flexible stance toward New Deal programs. The fact that the Supreme Court began approving laws similar to those which they had rejected just months ago irritated some of Hughes's colleagues. After the Court reversed its previous trend and approved measures such as Social Security and a minimum wage law, Justice Harlan Stone complained that Supreme Court decisions were becoming like "excursion tickets, good for this day and trip only." But by his combination of both standing up to Roosevelt and accommodating him, Hughes steered the Court through a perilous time.

Hughes presided over the Court for nearly 12 years before retiring on July 1, 1941. He lived for seven more years before his death on August 17, 1948. During his term as chief justice, Hughes impressed his colleagues as a fair yet decisive leader. Although he thought the Supreme Court carried more authority when it spoke with one voice, he encouraged his colleagues to dissent as they saw fit. Like a true umpire, he refused to let personal feelings cloud the issues. When Hugo Black joined the Court, Hughes welcomed him warmly even though Senator Black had voted against Hughes's confirmation as chief justice.

Charles Evans Hughes was both mocked and praised for being everything from a flaming liberal to an arch-conservative. The wide range of response is a good indication that Hughes favored no one. His legacy is that of a true umpire, a clear-sighted individual who kept the game running smoothly by simply calling the plays as he saw them.

Justice Hugo Black rose above the bitter prejudice and racial hatred of his native Deep South to become one of the country's foremost defenders of civil rights.

Chapter 7

Hugo Black:
Champion of the Underdog

*H*ugo Black's ride through the Senate confirmation hearings in 1937 had hit some rough bumps, but he had survived the questioning. The Senate had disregarded complaints that Black was too inexperienced to serve on the Supreme Court, that he was a Franklin Roosevelt "yes man" who had gone so far as to vote in favor of Roosevelt's Court-packing scheme. By a vote of 63-16, the Senate confirmed its colleague from Alabama.

Breathing a sigh of relief, Black set sail with his wife on a European vacation, glad that the worst was behind him. Little did he suspect that the worst was yet to come. While the Blacks were away, a reporter for the *Pittsburgh Post-Gazette* dug up a shocking skeleton from Black's past. In a Pulitzer Prize-winning article, the reporter revealed that Black had once been a member of the Ku Klux Klan, an organization with a history of violent discrimination against minorities. Black returned home to find the country in an uproar over the possibility of a cross-burning, white-hooded radical sitting on the highest court in the land.

Black went on radio to confront the issue. Speaking to the largest radio audience ever, he explained that the newspaper's "scoop" was hardly a dark secret. Voters in Alabama had known about it for years. "I did join the Klan," said Black, simply. "I later resigned. I never rejoined." He pointed to his strong record of support for civil rights as a senator and reminded listeners that the Klan had opposed him in the Senate election. Having made his statement, Black declared the issue closed and refused to say any more about it.

The furor over Black's nomination to the Supreme Court reminded some of the heated debate surrounding Brandeis's nomination. A newspaper editorial in Montgomery, Alabama, noted that the unpopular choice of Brandeis had turned out to be a brilliant move. "What a joke it would be," said the editorial, if the much-maligned Black turned into another great justice.

Sure enough, Black provided the punch line. Those who feared that Black would trample on individual rights looked on sheepishly as Black became the most determined and skilled defender of those liberties ever to sit on the Court. During his 34 years as a Supreme Court justice, the force of his convictions helped shake the Court loose from previous positions. More than once, a stirring minority opinion written by Black early in his career helped keep an issue alive until it gained a majority on the Court and became the law of the land.

Black was able to sympathize so easily with the underdog simply because he was one. Unlike the previous judges in this book, Black grew up alongside poverty, in close contact with the unfortunate and disadvantaged. Hugo LaFayette Black was born on February 27, 1886, in a farmhouse at Harlan, Alabama, the youngest of William and Martha Black's eight children. A few years after Hugo's birth, the family moved to the small town of Ashland, Alabama, where William Black made a decent living as a county merchant and farmer.

Hugo's education was not tightly structured. One school that he attended employed only one teacher for the first four grades. But he enjoyed learning math and reading and was especially attracted to politics and law. Hugo took after his father and became a loyal "Democat" before he could pronounce the party's name. In his memoirs, he pointed to Grover Cleveland's victory in the 1892 election as the sweetest memory of his life. The legal system fascinated Hugo so much that he regularly sat in on court sessions even as a small boy.

Without giving much thought to a career, Black followed his brother, Orlando, into the study of medicine. Medical school was easier for him to get into than college at that time, and so he entered a medical school in Birmingham in 1903. A tireless worker, Black studied seven days a week in order to cram two years of study into one. But during his second year at medical school, he woke up to the fact that he was not really interested in medicine. Returning to the subject that had always fascinated him, he entered law school at the University of Alabama.

Black completed law school in 1906, the same year that his mother died. His father had died some years earlier, and so the baby of the family suddenly found himself on his own. He returned to the familiarity of Ashland to start his law practice. Black had no chance to ease into the job. His first client was a black man accused of murder. The evidence was overwhelming, and Black lost the case, although he did save the man from a death sentence.

There was scant need for lawyers in that rural community, so Black earned little money. But working in a small town among people he knew forced Black to take on a wide variety of cases. Many of his clients were poor and had little education. Black had to learn to explain the law to them in plain English rather than specialized legal jargon.

In 1907 Black's law office burned down. The young lawyer headed to Birmingham, flat broke, to seek a better career. By accepting a variety of clients, from black sharecroppers to striking union workers, Black built a practice. He eventually worked his way into local government and served as a part-time judge in police court. He became known for his fast, but fair work—he once disposed of 118 cases in less than three hours!

Black won election as district attorney in Birmingham in 1914. The combination of eloquence and honesty made him a tough courtroom opponent. However, many of his actions upset the city's leading citizens. Believing it was as much his "duty to protect the innocent as to convict the guilty," he launched an investigation of police brutality in a local jail. He stopped the common police practice of setting up traps for poor laborers on payday so they could be arrested for gambling. He prosecuted a white man for the murder of a black. Although Black was criticized and threatened with impeachment, he continued to run his office according to his principles.

Black did not favor the involvement of the United States in World War I. But when his country entered the war, he joined the army. The war ended, however, before his artillery regiment shipped out to Europe.

Black returned home to marry Josephine Foster and to plot his next career move.

In 1926 he ran for the United States Senate as "the poor man's candidate." Visiting every city in Alabama in his Model T Ford, he won the hearts of the common people and easily captured the election. As a senator, he continued to side with the underdog. Big business corporations both feared and hated him for his tough investigation of business lobbying. When Roosevelt

Small-town Alabama lawyer Hugo Black won election to the U.S. Senate by speaking the plain language of the common people, whom he had long represented in his law practice.

became president, Black took a leading role in guiding the New Deal legislation through Congress.

In 1937 Roosevelt appointed him to fill the Supreme Court vacancy left by Willis Van Devanter. Although he regretted losing Black's voice in Congress, Roosevelt thought Black could be even more valuable on the Court.

Black agreed completely with Holmes that judges should keep their personal views out of their decisions. Black declared, "I shall not at any time surrender my belief that the document [the Constitution] itself should

Early in his second term, President Franklin Roosevelt tried, unsuccessfully, to influence the Court by packing it with more than nine justices. Eight of Roosevelt's nominees eventually reached the Court, including his first selection, the liberal-minded senator, Hugo Black.

be our guide, not our concept of what is fair, decent, or right." But he stubbornly opposed Holmes's call for flexibility in the law. "I cannot consider the Bill of Rights to be an outworn eighteenth century strait jacket," he insisted. Few, if any, judges have been as rigid as Black in applying the words of the Constitution to modern cases. For example, the First Amendment clause that applies to religion states that "Congress shall make no law respecting an establishment of religion, or prohibiting the free exercise thereof." While legal scholars debated just what those words meant, Black had no doubts. "No law means no law," he stated, and he consistently voted to strike down any laws that involved the government in religious matters.

Black took an equally narrow view of the right of free speech. He did not buy the "clear-and-present-danger" argument made by Holmes. As Black understood the Bill of Rights, American citizens were guaranteed an almost unlimited right to say whatever was on their mind. Yet he refused to extend that unlimited protection to protest marches and demonstrations, which many legal scholars considered an exercise of free speech. According to Black, speech meant spoken words, not actions.

After Black began work on the Court in August 1937, he spent a few years feeling his way before he warmed to his role as defender of the underdog. At first he felt intimidated by colleagues such as renowned law professor Felix Frankfurter, who believed in giving legislatures great freedom to make laws. In 1940, Black blindly followed Frankfurter's opinion that state law could require students to recite the Pledge of Allegiance to the flag every day. A few years later, Black made an even more glaring exception to his usual support of the powerless in the *Korematsu v. United States* case. Black wrote the majority opinion supporting the government's right to place Japanese-Americans in detention camps during World War II.

Both Black and another strong civil rights champion, William Douglas, kicked themselves for the 1940 flag salute decision. They came to believe that the idea of forcing people to swear an oath against their religious beliefs was a clear violation of the Bill of Rights. When a similar case reached the Court in 1943, Black and Douglas reversed themselves with a vengeance. Together with newly appointed members of the Court, they fashioned a majority opinion that declared such flag salute requirements unconstitutional.

That same year, Black issued what many regard as his most eloquent opinion. The case, *Chambers v. Florida*, involved four black men who were held and questioned around the clock for several days until they finally confessed to a murder. The Supreme Court overruled their conviction on the grounds that forced confessions violated the Constitution. Writing for the majority, Black said, "Under our constitutional system, courts stand against any winds that blow as havens of

William O. Douglas (1898-1980) served on the Court longer than any other justice—from 1939 to 1975. He was an outspoken conservationist and, like Justice Black, a steadfast defender of the First Amendment rights to free speech and a free press.

refuge for those who might otherwise suffer because they are helpless, weak, outnumbered, or because they are nonconforming victims of prejudice and public excitement."

Black regarded his 1947 dissent in *Adamson v. California* as his most important opinion. In that 5-4 decision, the Court ruled that federal constitutional rights, such as the right to remain silent, did not apply to state courts. Black protested that the Fourteenth Amendment made the Bill of Rights apply to all state laws as well as to federal laws. In declaring his strong support of the Constitution, Black said that the central issue was whether Americans would "try fearfully and futilely to preserve democracy by adopting totalitarian methods, or whether in accord with our traditions and our Constitution, we will have the confidence and courage to be free."

Black, however, found little support from his colleagues on the Court during the late 1940s and early 1950s. His opinions brought him a bombardment of scorn and abuse from many of the ordinary people he was trying to protect. After his opinion in the 1943 flag salute case, Black was called a "Bolshevik" and a "pinko" (Communist sympathizer). His sense of loneliness and isolation grew more acute when his wife died in 1951. In that year, Black lost another case concerning free speech. In *Dennis v. United States*, the Court upheld the conviction of a group of Communists who had been convicted of advocating the overthrow of the American government. In arguing for freedom of speech even for those with unpopular views, Black resigned himself to defeat even as he openly longed for brighter days. "Public opinion being what it now is, few will protest the conviction of these Communist petitioners. There is hope, however, that in calmer times, this or some later Court will restore First Amendment liberties where they belong in a free society."

In 1954 Black invited further criticism when he joined the Court in ordering schools to desegregate—to stop putting students in separate schools according to their race. Even many of his old friends considered him a traitor for that decision.

But the friend of the underdog held his ground. He began to rally in the mid-1950s, bolstered by his 1957 marriage to Elizabeth Seay Demeritte. New appointees to the Supreme Court began to side with Black and gradually extended all the guarantees of the Bill of Rights to the states.

In two key cases, Black clung firmly to his convictions until the Court came around to his way of thinking. In the 1942 case of *Betts v. Brady*, Black disagreed when the Court ruled that a state did not have to provide a poor person with a lawyer. "No man shall be deprived of counsel merely because of his poverty," Black argued. Twenty-one years later the case of *Gideon v. Wainwright* reached the Court. Clarence Gideon was a petty thief convicted of breaking and entering a pool hall. From his prison cell, Gideon had written to the Supreme Court, complaining that he had been too poor to hire a lawyer for his defense.

This time the Supreme Court agreed with Black that a competent defense against criminal charges was more than a privilege of the rich. It was a right of every American. The principle has never been seriously challenged since.

In the 1946 case of *Colegrove v. Green*, the majority of the Court voted not to get involved with matters of state voting laws, even when the districts were not divided equally according to population. Black's dissent, calling for the courts to enforce a "one-person, one-vote" principle of representation, was adopted as the law of the land in the 1960s.

Never one to back down from his convictions, Black spoke for the majority in several controversial cases involving religion. He first staked out his position on keeping religion and government separate in 1947. Perhaps the most famous of the freedom of religion cases was *Engel v. Vitale* in 1962. This concerned a nondenominational prayer that the New York State Board of Education recommended for students in public schools to recite each day. Officials hoped to avoid separation of church and state issues by saying that no one had to participate in the prayer if he did not want to. Parents of ten students, however, took the issue to the Supreme Court.

The majority of Court justices ruled that the prayer violated the First Amendment. Writing for the majority opinion, Black said, "The first and most immediate purpose of the amendment rested on the belief that a union of government and religion tends to destroy government and degrade religion."

Many Americans were outraged at what they saw as an attack on religion. Senator Sam Ervin of North Carolina went so far as to declare that the "Supreme Court has made God unconstitutional." Black, however, insisted, "It is neither sacrilegious nor antireligious to say that each separate government in this country should stay out of the business of writing or sanctioning prayers and leave that purely religious function to the people themselves and to those the people choose to look to for religious guidance."

Throughout his long career, Black displayed rare energy and stamina. Staff aides more than a generation younger dreaded walking onto a tennis court with the old judge, who routinely liked to go four or five sets before calling it a day.

Yet despite his enthusiasm and stubborn conviction, Black was one of most soft-spoken and polite justices on the Court. He kept a detailed book of anyone who had ever contributed to his political campaigns so that he could thank them if he met them. A gentleman to the end, he was proud of the fact that he "never wrote a word of discredit to my brothers" on the Court.

Hugo Black saved his passion for his work. He felt so strongly about constitutional rights that even later in life he could not read his *Chambers v. Florida* decision without weeping. He carried a copy of the Constitution in his pocket from the time he was confirmed to the day he resigned from the Court on September 17, 1971, one week before his death.

Nothing in Earl Warren's past would have suggested that his Court would make the most sweeping changes in social policy that Americans had ever seen.

Chapter 8

Earl Warren:
The Bland Revolutionary

*T*he Supreme Court's society-shaking decisions of the 1950s and 1960s prompted a storm of protest. So great was public anger that presidential candidates won votes by making the Supreme Court a major issue in the 1968 presidential campaign. Candidates ridiculed judges as "pointy-headed intellectuals" who sat in their ivory towers with their books, spouting philosophy and theories, isolated from the real world. Many Americans thought the Supreme Court needed judges with less book learning and more common sense. The legal system seemed to cry out for more practical leaders who understood everyday Americans, who stood for decency, who knew how to deal with criminals, and who could sympathize with the victims of crime.

Ironically, one man on the Court who fit almost every quality on the critics' wish list was the man they most despised: Chief Justice Earl Warren. Warren seemed to take pride in being a bland, ordinary guy. Unlike most of the other justices in this book, Warren was neither an exceptional student nor a widely respected legal scholar. His writing skill was average at best. Unlike Holmes, who enjoyed evenings of intellectual discussion, Warren felt he was not doing his job unless he was accomplishing something.

Warren came from a poor, working-class family. His common sense and basic decency so impressed voters that he managed the almost unheard of feat of winning both the Democratic and Republican primaries in the California race for governor. He understood the criminal mind well enough to become one of the country's most successful prosecutors. No one could claim that Warren did not understand the suffering of crime victims. His own father was murdered, and the person who did it was never brought to justice.

Warren's critics made a common mistake in misjudging the judge. President Dwight Eisenhower, too, thought he knew what he was getting when he put Warren on the Supreme Court. He later regretted this decision and thought of it as the worst mistake of his

President Dwight Eisenhower (1890-1969), a Republican whose views were generally described as conservative, was surprised to discover that his Supreme Court nominee, Earl Warren, was the most liberal chief justice in history.

presidency. Eisenhower failed to detect that Warren's easygoing personality and solid résumé masked a set of strong convictions. Warren's uncanny skill in putting those convictions into action produced what one observer called "a revolution made by judges." Abandoning the caution of previous courts, the Warren Court took an active role in shaping American society.

Earl Warren was born in Los Angeles, California, on

March 19, 1891, to Methias and Christine Warren. Both parents were Scandinavian immigrants who had moved to California in 1889. The Warrens' lives were controlled by the Southern Pacific Railroad, which dominated the state government and employed Methias as a maintenance worker. When Methias joined a strike against the company in 1894, Southern Pacific made it impossible for him to find any work in Los Angeles. The Warrens then moved to Bakersfield, California.

Methias Warren, bitter over his treatment, insisted that his children escape his lot in life by getting a good education. Earl worked hard at his studies, although he was never an outstanding student. He attended public schools through high school and went to the University of California at Berkeley. After completing his undergraduate work, he stayed at the school to study law.

Warren picked up his father's resentment of authority, especially when he saw how little the Southern Pacific cared about its workers whose legs were cut off in railroad accidents. Occasionally, he expressed that rebellious nature. While at law school, he refused to speak in class for an entire year as a protest against the way a course was being taught.

Warren so enjoyed the northern California climate that he set up his law practice there in 1914 after completing his studies. The involvement of the United States in World War I interrupted his career. Warren, who remained intensely patriotic all his life, joined the army in 1917. Like Hugo Black, he never saw action, and his two years of training recruits for combat in Europe were mostly boring.

Shortly after returning from the military, Warren landed a position as a clerk for the California legislature. That humble beginning launched Warren into a spectacularly successful career in government. Beginning with his campaign for district attorney of Alameda County in 1925, Warren won every election that he entered. During his 14 years as district attorney, Warren displayed the superb administrative and organization skills that had never been apparent in school. His record of efficient, able prosecutions discouraged any challenger from running against him in 1930 and 1934.

At the same time, he witnessed the kind of government corruption that added to his old suspicion of authority. Police were taking bribes and committing other crimes to cover their tracks. Political bosses were rewarding their cronies and ignoring the public interest. Determined to stay independent of corrupt influences, Warren refused to answer to anyone but the voters. He avoided politics by not supporting candidates from either party in elections and by making a practice of entering both Democratic and Republican primaries. In 1938 Warren won the Democratic, Republican, and Progressive party primaries in his race for California attorney general.

As attorney general, Warren was credited with

Japanese-Americans at the Tule Lake internment camp in Newell, California. As California's attorney general in 1942, Earl Warren helped to write one of the most shameful chapters in American history—the denial of a group's constitutional rights that allowed rounding up, detaining, and relocating people based solely on their national origin.

establishing a higher standard of professional conduct among police. He also led the drive during World War II to move all Japanese, even those who were American citizens, from California to detention camps further east. Reflecting the West Coast racism in which he was raised, he argued, "If the Japs are released, no one will be able to tell a saboteur from any other Jap." No official disputed him and the relocation program went forward. Later, he expressed deep regret for his actions.

Warren had no political ambitions beyond being attorney general. He and his wife, Nina, a widow whom he had married in 1925, did not want any added pressures while raising their six children through their school years. But after four years of being snubbed by the state's Democratic governor, Culbert Olson, a seething Warren could stand no more. Campaigning on the slogan of "Leadership, Not Politics," he captured the Republican nomination in 1942 and then defeated Olson.

Warren worked hard as governor to bring about needed changes in public health, higher education, and California's prisons. His sweeping victory for a second term in 1946 so impressed the national Republican party that they asked him to run for vice-president of the United States. Warren agreed reluctantly and was almost relieved when his presidential running mate, Thomas Dewey, lost the 1948 election to Harry Truman.

Warren won a third term as governor in 1950 by more than a million votes, a triumph that brought him serious consideration as a candidate for president. The 1952 Republican convention, however, settled into a two-man race between General Dwight Eisenhower and Senator Robert Taft. As the leader of the California delegation, Warren helped swing his state's votes to Eisenhower.

143

Shortly after winning the presidency, Eisenhower saw a chance to return the favor. Supreme Court Chief Justice Fred Vinson died suddenly of a heart attack on September 8, 1953. Feeling safe with Warren's moderate stance on issues and his rare combination of high ideals and common sense, Eisenhower nominated Warren to take Vinson's place.

The new chief justice wasted little time in showing the strength that lay beneath that friendly, bland exterior. In 1954 the Court was wrestling with the case of *Brown v. The Board of Education of Topeka*. Oliver Brown, a black minister, had filed suit to allow his daughter to attend a whites-only elementary school in Topeka. At that time Kansas was one of 17 states that required their public schools to be segregated. Following Harlan's tradition rather than Holmes's, Warren was swayed as much by his own sense of right and wrong as by legal arguments. His questioning of those who testified before the Court often strayed from technical points into moral questions such as "Why did you treat him this way?" Warren was not impressed by the fact that the 1896 case of *Plessy v. Ferguson* had established "separate but equal" as the law of the land. For him, the Brown case was a simple matter of racial injustice, and the Court's job was to see that justice prevailed.

Unlike Harlan, however, Warren had a gift for getting people with conflicting ideas to work together. Despite his unassuming appearance, he had an air of

The Reverend Oliver Brown, 12 addtitional plaintiffs, and the Topeka branch of the National Association for the Advancement of Colored People (NAACP) filed the law-suit that became Brown v. The Board of Education of Topeka.

The Supreme Court ruled that Linda Brown (left), and black children nationwide could attend public schools that until then had been open to whites only.

authority about him that commanded the respect of his colleagues. Some historians suspect that the Court would have rejected Brown's suit had Vinson remained chief justice. But Warren not only got the Court to overturn *Plessy v. Ferguson*, he also added weight to the decision by getting a unanimous verdict. He fashioned that agreement by avoiding accusing and emotional language and by giving in to his colleagues on minor points. For example, at Justice Frankfurter's request, Warren's opinion required school systems to desegregate "with all deliberate speed," a phrase meant to soothe those who feared too rapid a change.

In his decision, Warren ruled that forced segregation of schools violated the equal protection provisions of the Constitution. He declared that "separate but equal" educational facilities were, by their very nature, unequal. "School segregation by state law causes a feeling of inferiority in black children that inflicts damage to their hearts and minds that may never be undone," he wrote. Therefore, "we conclude that in the field of public education, the doctrine of separate but equal has no place."

In a bold stroke, the Court had shaken the foundation of legalized racism in the United States. With the weight of the Supreme Court behind it, the civil rights movement gained momentum through the 1960s. All during the struggle, the Warren Court hammered away at racial barriers. It ruled unanimously that Congress had acted within its constitutional rights by requiring desegregation of all public facilities in the Civil Rights Act of 1964. In 1967 the Court declared that state laws forbidding interracial marriage violated the Fourteenth Amendment to the Constitution.

Steadily, the Warren Court plunged into battles with other government branches. In the 1957 case of *Watkins v. United States*, the Court rushed to the defense of individuals hauled before bullying Senate committees. Watkins, a former union official, testified before the House UnAmerican Activities Committee that he had at one time cooperated with the Communist party. When he refused to reveal the names of Communists, the House charged him with contempt of Congress. The Supreme Court dismissed the case. According to Warren, the committee had violated Watkins's Fifth Amendment rights against self-incrimination. Warren refused to allow the "ruthless exposure of private lives by a committee defining its own authority."

In the 1960s the Court took on issues of voting restrictions and boundaries. Traditionally, courts had refused to muddy themselves by getting into the political infighting connected with these issues. But the Warren Court used the case of *Reynolds v. Sims* in 1964 to strike what it saw as another blow for justice. In the Reynolds case, voters in six states filed suit against their legislatures' practice of dividing the state's voting districts according to land area rather than population. The Supreme Court ruled in favor of the voters and declared that voting districts for legislative bodies in every state must be divided strictly on the basis of population.

"Legislature represents people, not acres or trees," explained Warren in his decision. "The weight of a citizen's vote cannot be made to depend on where he lives." Warren considered this "one-person-one-vote" ruling his Court's most important action against special interest groups.

The Court produced another landmark decision in the case of *New York Times Company v. Sullivan* in 1964. The dispute involved an advertisement in *The New York Times* sponsored by civil rights advocates who were appealing for contributions following the arrest of Martin Luther King, Jr., in Montgomery, Alabama. The ad contained some statements, not all of which were totally accurate, that a Montgomery official named L. B. Sullivan considered a personal attack. Claiming that his reputation had been libeled, he sued for damages and won his case in the lower courts.

The Supreme Court, however, overruled the earlier verdicts on grounds that the advertisement was protected by the clause in the Bill of Rights that guaranteed freedom of the press. In order to encourage free and open debate on public issues, the Court said that government officials could sue newspapers for libel only if they could prove that the newspaper knew its statements were false or acted with reckless disregard for the truth.

Of all the Warren Court's historic decisions, the one

that most stuck in the public's craw was the 1966 verdict in *Miranda v. Arizona*. Ernesto Miranda was convicted of kidnapping and raping a Phoenix woman, and sentenced to 20 to 30 years in prison. His lawyers appealed the verdict because the police had forced him to incriminate himself.

As a prosecutor and a district attorney, Warren had seen too many cases of police abusing their authority. Realizing that innocent people could suffer at the mercy of such police, Warren sought a way to protect the public. In the Miranda case, decided by the narrowest of margins in favor of Miranda, Warren offered a way. Warren not only ordered a retrial for Miranda but also spelled out exactly what a police officer must do to protect the rights of citizens. This included warning them at the time of arrest that they had the right to remain silent and to consult with an attorney before answering questions.

As in many Supreme Court cases, the decision made little difference to the people directly involved. Miranda was convicted again at his retrial. But the Miranda decision had a larger impact on society. People said that these Supreme Court justices were soft on crime and that they cared more for the rights of criminals than for those of victims. Politicians who promised a return to "law and order" made the Court decision a major election issue.

Despite Warren's tremendous impact on American

society, his name is probably most commonly associated with something that had nothing to do with the Supreme Court. The confusion surrounding President Kennedy's assassination in 1963 sparked fears that the slaying had been part of a larger conspiracy. To lay doubts to rest, the new president, Lyndon Johnson, persuaded Warren, whom he called "the personification of fairness," to head a commission to investigate the assassination.

A military honor guard carries the body of slain U.S. President John F. Kennedy (1917-1963) to lie in state in Washington, D.C. The findings of the Warren Commission, which investigated Kennedy's assassination, are widely debated to this day.

150

Warren called this work "a most unpleasant experience." Lack of cooperation from the FBI and the CIA made the task difficult. The Warren Commission concluded that Lee Harvey Oswald had acted alone in shooting the president and reported no evidence of a conspiracy. But the report failed to settle the issue. The debate over who killed John Kennedy continues to rage.

Although a skilled group leader, Warren did not care much for socializing. He jealously guarded his private time with his family. Rarely did he invite others to his home or accept invitations offered by others. When the duties of his office required it, he shared his opinions, but otherwise kept them to himself. Except for his selective memoirs, written after he resigned from the Court in 1969, Warren left no written evidence of his thoughts during his life.

But by the time he died of a heart attack on July 9, 1974, his dynamic leadership had left a deep imprint on American society. Many have questioned whether Warren was wise in promoting such an active role for the Court in molding society. His tactics have opened the door for judges with entirely different values to exercise the same influence on society. The Warren Court went so far out in front of society that his successors have been retreating from some of its stances ever since.

In response to critics who complained that the Court was getting involved where it had no business to be, Warren argued that "the Court sits to decide cases, not to avoid decision." He insisted that the theory "when in doubt, don't" frequently kept justice from being done. For Earl Warren, upholding justice was the whole reason for having a Supreme Court. In his laid-back, bland style, Earl Warren used the power of the Court to elevate his concept of justice to the law of the land.

Justices of the Supreme Court Fact Sheet

Justice & Home State	Birth & Death	Appointment by	Court Term
John Marshall* Virginia	b. Sept. 24, 1755 d. July 6, 1835	John Adams	Jan. 27, 1801 to July 6, 1835
Roger Taney* Maryland	b. Mar. 17, 1777 d. Oct. 12, 1864	Andrew Jackson	Mar. 15, 1836 to Oct. 12, 1864
John Harlan Kentucky	b. June 1, 1833 d. Oct. 14, 1911	Rutherford B. Hayes	Nov. 29, 1877 to Oct. 14, 1911
Oliver Wendell Holmes Massachusetts	b. Mar. 8, 1841 d. Mar. 6, 1935	Theodore Roosevelt	Dec. 4, 1902 to Jan. 12, 1932
Louis Brandeis Massachusetts	b. Nov. 13, 1856 d. Oct. 5, 1941	Woodrow Wilson	June 1, 1916 to Feb. 13, 1939
Charles Evans Hughes** New York	b. April 11, 1862 d. Aug. 27, 1948	William H. Taft Herbert Hoover	May 2, 1910 to June 10, 1916 Feb. 13, 1930 to July 1, 1941
Hugo Black Alabama	b. Feb. 27, 1886 d. Sept. 25, 1971	Franklin D. Roosevelt	August 17, 1937 to Sept. 17, 1971
Earl Warren* California	b. Mar. 19, 1891 d. July 9, 1974	Dwight D. Eisenhower	Mar. 1, 1954 to June 23, 1969

*Chief Justice
**Chief Justice in second term

Bibliography

Abraham, Henry J. *Justices and Presidents.* London: Oxford University Press, 1985.

Asch, Sidney H. *The Supreme Court And Its Great Justices.* New York: ARCO, 1971.

Baker, Leonard. *John Marshall: A Life in Law.* New York: Macmillan, 1974.

Bernstein, Richard and Jerome Agel. *The Supreme Court: Into the Third Century.* New York: Walker, 1989.

Black, Hugo L. and Elizabeth. *Mr. Justice and Mrs. Black: The Memoirs of Hugo L. Black and Elizabeth Black.* New York: Random House, 1986.

Friedman, Leon and Fred L. Israel, ed. *The Justices of the United States Supreme Court, 1789-1978, vol. 1-5.* New York: Chelsea House, 1980.

Latham, Frank. *The Great Dissenter.* New York: Cowles Book Company, 1970.

Lawson, Don. *Landmark Supreme Court Cases.* Hillside, New Jersey: Enslow Publishers, 1987.

Novick, Sheldon M. *Honorable Justice: The Life of Oliver Wendell Holmes.* Boston: Little, Brown and Company, 1989.

Rehnquist, William H. *The Supreme Court: How It Was, How It Is.* New York: William Morrow, 1987.

Severn, Bill. *John Marshall: The Man Who Made The Court Supreme.* New York: David McKay and Company, 1969.

Strum, Philippa. *Louis D. Brandeis: Justice for the People.* Cambridge, Massachusetts: Harvard University Press, 1984.

Weiss, Ann E. *The Supreme Court.* Hillside, New Jersey: Enslow Publishers, 1987.

White, G. Edward. *Earl Warren: A Public Life.* New York and London: Oxford University Press, 1982.

Witt, Elder, ed. *Congressional Quarterly's Guide to the United States Supreme Court.* Washington, D.C.: Congressional Quarterly, 1979.

Wormser, Michael. *The Supreme Court: Justice and the Law.* Washington, D.C.: Congressional Quarterly, 1983.

INDEX

Photo Credits

Photographs courtesy of Library of Congress: pp. 8, 11, 13, 15, 16, 18, 19, 21, 23, 28, 31, 34, 36, 38, 45 (all), 47, 51, 53, 54, 63, 70, 74, 78, 83, 86, 93, 96, 102, 111, 115, 116, 120, 126, 127, 130, 136, 139, 142, 150, back cover; Illinois State Historical Library, p. 60; University of Louisville Archives, pp. 90 (both), 99; Minnesota Historical Society, pp. 108, 112, 117; Brown & Brown Associates, p. 145 (both).